Better Homes and Gardens®

AFGHANS TO KNIT & CROCHET

BETTER HOMES AND GARDENS® BOOKS

Editor: Gerald M. Knox
Art Director: Ernest Shelton
Managing Editor: David A. Kirchner
Copy and Production Editors: James D. Blume,
   Marsha Jahns, Rosanne Weber Mattson,
   Mary Helen Schiltz

Crafts Editor: Jean LemMon
Senior Crafts Books Editor: Joan Cravens
Associate Crafts Books Editors: Sara Jane Treinen,
   Judith Veeder

Associate Art Directors: Linda Ford Vermie,
   Neoma Alt West, Randall Yontz
Assistant Art Directors: Lynda Haupert,
   Harijs Priekulis, Tom Wegner
Senior Graphic Designers: Jack Murphy, Stan Sams,
   Darla Whipple-Frain
Graphic Designers: Mike Burns, Sally Cooper,
   Brian Wignall, Kim Zarley

Vice President, Editorial Director: Doris Eby
Executive Director, Editorial Services: Duane L. Gregg

President, Book Group: Fred Stines
Director of Publishing: Robert B. Nelson
Vice President, Retail Marketing: Jamie Martin
Vice President, Direct Marketing: Arthur Heydendael

AFGHANS TO KNIT AND CROCHET
Crafts Editors: Joan Cravens, Sara Jane Treinen
Contributing Editor: Gary Boling
Copy and Production Editor: Marsha Jahns
Graphic Designer: Mike Burns
Electronic Text Processor: Donna Russell

Cover project: See pages 8 and 9.

CONTENTS

Fun to Make Scrap-Saver Designs —————— 4

Leftovers never looked better than in the afghans
shown in this section. Here are seven designs to knit
or crochet from scraps, plus tips and techniques to
help you make creative (and thrifty) use of even the
smallest bits of yarn in your workbasket.

Patchwork Patterns
For Afghans and Throws —————————— 20

Flying Geese, Log Cabin, and Irish Chain are just a few
of the patterns inspired by American quilts that you
will find adapted for knitting and crocheting in this
chapter. If you share the enthusiasm and admiration
of many crafters for traditional patchwork designs,
you're sure to find an afghan or two that you can
stitch with pleasure and display with pride.

Classic Favorites in Both Techniques ——— 46

How often have you wanted to knit an afghan only to
discover it was crocheted, or wished you had crochet
instructions for a favorite knitted design? In this
chapter you will find time-honored favorites—ripples,
checks, plaids, argyles, and popular Aran patterns—in
both techniques. Whether you knit or crochet, you can
stitch these designs easily.

Stitcher's Notebook ————————————— 72

Here are crocheting and knitting abbreviations, stitch
instructions, and helpful hints to ensure successful
completion of the projects in this book.

Acknowledgments ————————————— 80

SCRAP-SAVER DESIGNS

♦ ♦ ♦

Like a magician's bag of tricks, a stitcher's workbasket is the source of all manner of marvelous things. With a little imagination and a sense of adventure, you can turn even your scraps into an enchanting afghan or two. Here and on the next few pages are six designs to get you started. Of course, you can purchase yarns for each one, but the real fun is in combining yarns you already have to create stunning effects.

The sampler afghan, *right,* is a dabbler's delight. It's made from 42 eight-inch squares of knitted, crocheted, and woven fabrics whipstitched together and trimmed with a simple crocheted border.

For the hand-worked blocks, choose from seven knitted and four crocheted patterns. Work the squares in worsted-weight yarn. Then set off the scrap-yarn blocks with plaid, tweed, and solid-color woolen squares bound with buttonhole stitches. Tie this imaginative mix together with a multicolored border stitched in rounds.

The afghan shown measures 50x60 inches, but you can make your afghan any size, depending on the number of yarn and fabric scraps you have on hand. How-to instructions for the afghans in this section begin on page 14.

SCRAP-SAVER DESIGNS

The simplest way to stitch a scrap afghan is to work in stripes, either diagonally, as shown *opposite,* or horizontally, as shown at *right.*

Begin by dividing leftover yarns into color groups. Are your yarns primarily shades of one or two colors? Or do you have a sampling of go-together tints that would be suitable for a single project? These afghans are perfect for just such an assortment of yarns.

Five shades of blue and three neutrals—gray, cream, and white—are used for the 55x65-inch bias-stripe afghan, *opposite.*

Begin working this design with a double crochet shell. Increase one shell in each row until you've made a triangle with 85 shells on the longest side. Work even for 12 inches, then shape the throw into a rectangle by decreasing one shell in each row until only one shell remains.

To finish the afghan, work rounds of shells in each color around the edge.

The 44x63-inch, horizontally striped afghan, *above,* features a simple two-row texture pattern that enables you to change colors often—a bonus when you're working with scraps.

SCRAP-SAVER DESIGNS

Here's a variation on a simple stripe design that even a beginner can stitch with ease. Work the background in stockinette stitch (knit one row, purl one row), then add vertical rows of bold duplicate stitch embroidery in dynamic colors.

To finish this 50x60-inch throw, add a narrow border of single crochet and a lavish, multicolored fringe.

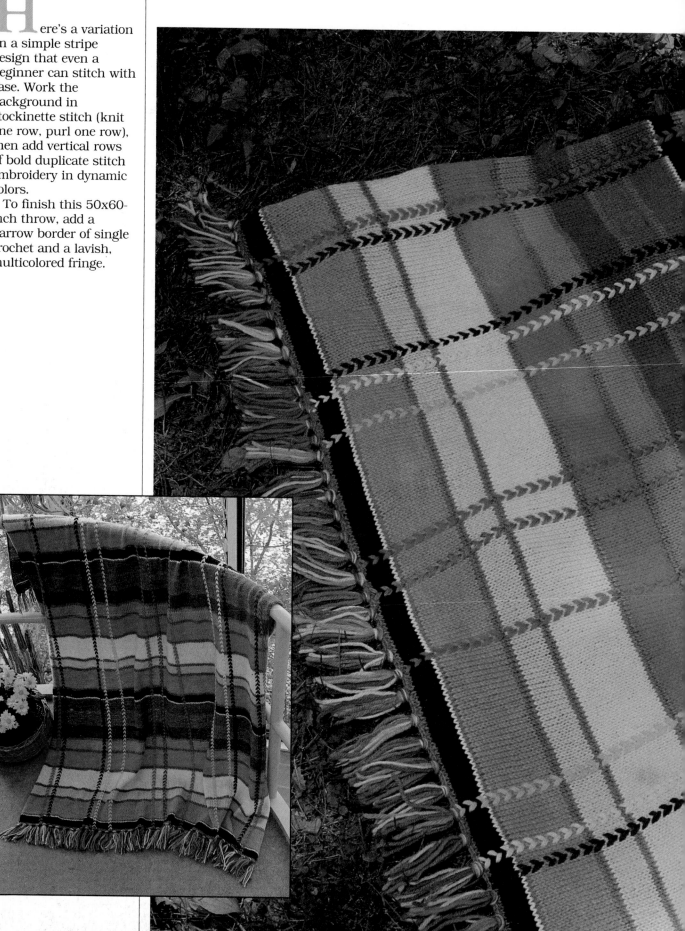

SCRAP-SAVER DESIGNS

Granny squares, and their countless variations, are the hands-down favorite of scrap-bag crocheters. This type of crochet, characterized by repeated motifs begun with a central ring and worked in concentric rounds, lends itself to working with scrap yarns because even short lengths of yarn can be put to good use.

The spectacular granny afghan, *opposite*, gains color impact from the three rounds of puff stitches used to form a wheel within each square. You can work the puff-stitch rounds in any combination of colors. In this 51x73-inch design, some squares are monochromatic, and some are worked in complementary shades. A liberal sprinkling of red throughout offsets the muted colors that edge the wheels.

A sprightly single crochet border, worked in taupes, grays, and red, features two rounds of gray and red stripes. A final round of red picots trims this fun-to-stitch design.

The granny squares in the 22½x29½-inch doll blanket, *above*, are stitched in the traditional fashion—from rounds of double crochet stitches. Use bits and pieces of sport yarn to stitch these 2½-inch squares, then assemble 63 of them into this special gift for a child.

One of the most imaginative—and thriftiest—ways of using even the smallest scraps of leftover yarn is to stitch them into the motifs found in Fair Isle knitting designs.

Named for the British island where it originated, Fair Isle knitting is also one of the most popular ways to introduce color and pattern into flat knitted panels. With this technique, you simply knit the patterns as you stitch each row, rather than adding the designs when the knitting is done.

The playful 48x60-inch afghan, *left*, features simple heart, flower, and bird motifs. You won't have to knit each of the 80 squares in the Fair Isle technique; some are solid colors or stripes.

Our charts show the basic patterns for the Fair Isle designs, but you can alter the patterns to make any number of delightful combinations. Before you begin, use graph paper and colored pencils to chart a knitted block. Then knit the design, row by row, to match the chart.

Make sure the motifs in your Fair Isle designs blend smoothly with background stitches by learning to maneuver the yarns correctly when you change colors.

First, when changing from one yarn color to another, drop the color in use to the back of the work. With the new color in hand, twist it around the color just used, then knit a stitch with the new color. This twisting of yarns prevents holes in the finished work.

Every three or four stitches, continue twisting the color in use around the color just used, so that yarn carried across the back of your work will not snag or become distorted. If the color areas are widely separated, using yarn bobbins will simplify this procedure.

SCRAP-SAVER DESIGNS

Sampler Afghan

Shown on pages 4 and 5.

Finished size is approximately 50x60 inches.

MATERIALS
Bernat Sesame "4" worsted yarn: Leftover amounts of No. 7533 red, No. 7565 navy, No. 7579 moss, No. 7512 gray, No. 7514 cinnamon, and No. 7540 oyster
8½x8½-inch wool fabric scraps in solids and plaids to match yarns
Size 8 knitting needle, or size to obtain gauge given below
Sizes H and I aluminum crochet hooks, or sizes to obtain gauge given below
Crewel needle

Abbreviations: See pages 73 and 77.
Gauge: With knitting needles over st st, 5 sts = 1 inch; 6 rows = 1 inch. With Size I crochet hook, 7 sc = 2 inches. Afghan blocks are 8x8 inches.

INSTRUCTIONS
Plan blocks to be worked for afghan using colors of your choice. (See instructions for knitted, crocheted, and fabric blocks below and refer to photograph on pages 4 and 5.) Our afghan is made of 42 blocks, 15 fabric blocks, 12 knitted blocks, and 15 crocheted blocks. Use all or select your favorite blocks to work the afghan.

For the knitted blocks
KNITTED BLOCK 1—garter stitch (make 1): Cast on 40 sts. K every row until block is square. Bind off.

KNITTED BLOCK 2—stockinette stitch (make 1): Cast on 40 sts. *Row 1:* K across.
Row 2: P across. Rep rows 1 and 2 until block is square. Bind off.

For striped block, make 1. Rep rows 1 and 2 for 10 rows for each color stripe, including the cast-on and bind-off rows. Bind off.

KNITTED BLOCK 3 (diamond stitch): Make 2. Cast on 40 sts.
Row 1: (K 4, p 1, k 3) 5 times.
Row 2: (P 2, k 1, p 1, k 1, p 3) 5 times.
Row 3: (K 2, p 1, k 3, p 1, k 1) 5 times.
Row 4: (K 1, p 5, k 1, p 1) 5 times.
Row 5: P 1, (k 7, p 1) 4 times, k 7.
Row 6: Work same as Row 4.
Row 7: Work same as Row 3.
Row 8: Work same as Row 2.
Rep rows 1-8 until block is square. Bind off.

KNITTED BLOCK 4 (wide garter rib): Make 1. Cast on 40 sts.
Row 1 (right side): K across.
Row 2: (K 5, p 2) 5 times; end k 5. Rep rows 1 and 2 until block is square. Bind off.
For striped block, make 1. Alternate colors every 8 rows.

KNITTED BLOCK 5 (basket weave): Make 2. Cast on 40 sts.
Rows 1–4: (K 5, p 5) 4 times.
Rows 5–8: (P 5, k 5) 4 times.
Rep rows 1–8 until block is square. Bind off.

KNITTED BLOCK 6 (mock cable): Make 2. Cast on 40 sts.
Row 1: P 1, * k 2, p 2; rep from * across, ending with k 2, p 1.
Row 2: K 1, * p 1, yo, p 1, k 2; rep from * across, ending with k 1.
Row 3: P 1, * k 3, p 2; rep from * across, ending with k 3, p 1.
Row 4: K 1, * p 3, k 2; rep from * across, ending with k 1.
Row 5: P 1, * sl first st as to k, k 2, psso, p 2; rep from * across, ending with p 1.
Rep rows 2-5 until block is square. Bind off.

KNITTED BLOCK 7 (fancy rib): Make 1. Cast on 41 sts.
Row 1: * K 3, p 1; rep from * across, ending with k 1.
Rep Row 1 until work is square. Bind off.

For the crocheted blocks
CROCHETED BLOCK 1 (single crochet stripe): Make 3. With Size I hook, ch 25.
Row 1: Sk first ch, sc in rem 24 ch across; ch 1, turn.
Row 2: Sc in each sc across; ch 1, turn. Rep Row 2, working 2 rows for each color stripe as desired until block is square.

CROCHETED BLOCK 2 (popcorn stripe): Make 4. With Size H hook, ch 29 loosely.
Row 1: Dc in fourth ch from hook and in next ch; **ch 1, 4 dc in next ch, drop hook from lp, insert hook under ch-1 sp preceding the 4 dc, pull dropped lp through, ch 1—popcorn (pc) made;** * dc in each of next 3 ch, pc in next ch. Rep from * across, dc in last 3 ch; ch 3, turn.
Row 2: Sk first dc, dc in each dc and in top of each pc across; dc in top of turning ch; ch 3, turn.
Row 3: Sk first dc, * pc in next dc, dc in each of next 3 dc. Rep from * across; ending pc in next dc, dc in top of ch-3; ch 3, turn.
Row 4: Work same as Row 2.
Row 5: Sk first dc, dc in each of next 2 dc, * pc in next dc, dc in next 3 dc. Rep from * across, ending pc in next dc, dc in next dc and top of turning-ch; ch 3, turn.
Rep rows 2-5 until 13 rows are worked, ending with pc row; fasten off.

CROCHETED BLOCK 3 (granny square): Make 4. With Size H hook, ch 5, join with sl st to form ring.
Rnd 1: Ch 3, 2 dc in ring, (ch 3, 3 dc in ring) 3 times; ch 3, join with sl st to top of beg ch-3. Fasten off.
Rnd 2: Join new color in any ch-3 sp; ch 3, in same sp work 2 dc, ch 3, 3 dc; (ch 1, in next ch-3 sp work 3 dc, ch 3, 3 dc) 3 times; ch 1, join to top of ch-3 at beg of rnd; fasten off.
Rnd 3: Join new color in any ch-3 corner sp; ch 3, in same sp work 2 dc, ch 3, 3 dc; (ch 1, 3 dc in

next ch-1 sp, ch 1; in next ch-3 corner sp work 3 dc, ch 3, 3 dc) 3 times; ch 1, 3 dc in next ch-1 sp, ch 1, join to top of ch-3 at beg of rnd; fasten off.

Rnd 4: Join new color in ch-3 corner sp; ch 3, in same sp work 2 dc, ch 3, 3 dc; * ch 1, (3 dc in next ch-1 sp, ch 1) twice; in corner sp work 3 dc, ch 3, 3 dc; rep from * 2 times more; ending ch 1, (3 dc in next ch-1 sp) twice, ch 1; join to top of ch-3 at beg of rnd; fasten off.

Rnds 5–7: Work same as for Rnd 4, but add 1 more 3-dc grp on sides of each rnd.

Rnd 8: Join new color in any ch-3 corner sp, ch 1, 3 sc in same sp, * (sc in next 3 dc and ch-1 st) 6 times, sc in next 3 dc; 3 sc in corner sp; rep from * around; join with sl st to first sc; fasten off.

CROCHETED BLOCK 4: (popcorn granny): Make 4. With Size I hook, ch 5, join with sl st to form ring.

Rnd 1: Ch 1, 8 sc in ring; join with sl st to first sc.

Rnd 2: Ch 3, 4 dc in same st as join, drop hook from work, insert hook in top of ch-3 at beg of rnd, pull dropped lp through, ch 1; * ch 2, in next sc **make 5 dc, drop hook from work, insert hook in first dc of 5-dc grp and pull dropped lp through, ch 1 tightly—popcorn (pc) made.** Rep from * around; end ch 2, join with sl st in first ch-2 sp.

Rnd 3: Ch 3, 3 dc in same sp; in *each* ch-2 sp around work 4 dc; join to top of beg ch-3.

Rnd 4: Note: For this rnd *only,* work in back lp of sts. Ch 3, in same place as sl st work dc, ch 2, 2 dc; * dc in each of next 2 dc, hdc in next dc, sc in next dc, hdc in next dc, dc in next 2 dc, in next dc make 2 dc, ch 2, 2 dc for corner. Rep from * around, ending in pat as established; join to top of ch-3 at beg of rnd.

Rnd 5: Sl st in next dc and into ch-2 sp, ch 3, in same sp make dc, ch 2, 2 dc; * dc in each of next 11 sts, in corner ch-2 sp make 2 dc, ch 2, 2 dc. Rep from * around, ending in pat as established and working last dc in first sl st at beg of rnd; join to top of ch-3.

Rnd 6: Sl st in next dc and into ch-2 sp, ch 3, in same sp make dc, ch 2, 2 dc; * (dc in next 3 dc, pc in next dc) 3 times; dc in next 3 dc; in corner sp make 2 dc, ch 2, 2 dc. Rep from * around, working last dc in first sl st at beg of rnd; join to top of ch-3.

Rnd 7: Work same as Rnd 5, making 19 dc along side in each dc *and* pc of previous rnd and working 2 dc, ch 2, 2 dc in each corner sp; join; fasten off. *Note:* If block needs to be larger, work 1 more rnd of dc or sc around, with 23 dc or sc on each side.

FINISHING BLOCKS: All of the blocks should measure 8x8 inches. If they are slightly smaller, work 1 or 2 rnds sc around to make them larger. If the blocks are too narrow, work sc along the short sides only.

When all blocks match, work a rnd of sc around both the knitted and the crocheted blocks, using either the same color as the block or a contrasting color, making 3 sc in corners.

For the fabric blocks

For each fabric block, cut 2 squares from wool to measure 8½x8½ inches (includes ¼-inch seam allowances). The 2 fabrics for each square need not match.

With right sides facing, stitch the squares together, leaving an opening for turning. Clip corners and turn right side out. Steam-press and slip-stitch the opening closed.

Thread a long strand of contrasting yarn through crewel needle and work blanket (also called buttonhole) stitch evenly spaced around all sides of fabric block, working through 1 thickness of the fabric only.

To make the assembly of the afghan easy, work the same number of blanket stitches on each side as there are scs on the sides of the knitted and crocheted blocks. When all blocks are completed, arrange in a pleasing manner. Whipstitch blocks together, sewing through blanket stitching of fabric blocks and sc of yarn blocks.

BORDER: Work 3 rnds (each a different color) around the outside edge of afghan, working 3 sc in each corner.

Bias-Striped Crocheted Afghan

Shown on page 6.

Finished size is 55x65 inches, including the border.

MATERIALS
Neveda Atlantis acrylic worsted-weight yarn (100-gram skeins): 2 skeins *each* of No. 9610 white, No. 9640 Cream, No. 9613 gray, No. 9636 medium blue, No. 9637 colonial blue, No. 9638 cornflower blue, No. 9639 dark blue, and No. 9656 light blue
Size G aluminum crochet hook, or size to obtain gauge given below

Abbreviations: See page 73.
Gauge: After 7 rows of work, afghan measures 4 inches along both short sides.

INSTRUCTIONS
Note: Colors are used randomly throughout afghan, with each color stripe worked in 1 color.

With any color, ch 4.

Row 1: Work 2 dc in fourth ch from hook; **work dc in same ch until 2 lps remain on hook, drop color in use, draw new color through 2 lps on hook—color**

continued

change made. With new color, ch 3, turn. *Note:* Make all color changes in the last dc of the row in this manner.

Row 2: **Work 2 dc in first dc—beg shell made;** sk 2 dc, **work 3 dc in top of turning ch—3 dc-shell made,** changing color in third dc, ch 3, turn.

Row 3: With new color, make beg shell in first dc, 3 dc-shell bet next 2 shell-grps, 3 dc-shell in top of turning ch-3, changing color in third dc—3 shells made; ch 3, turn.

Row 4: Work beg shell in first dc, (3 dc-shell bet next 2 shell-grps) twice; 3 dc in top of turning ch, changing color in third dc—4 shells made; ch 3, turn.

Rows 5–84: Rep Row 4, making 1 more shell than in previous row. Row 5 will have 5 shells in row. Row 6 will have 6 shells in row, and so on. Change colors randomly. *Note:* To facilitate hiding the yarn ends, carry the ends of each row along the work and crochet over them as you begin the next row.

Establish the rectangle shaping as follows:

Row 85: Work across row as established and make 84 shells; work just 1 dc in top of turning ch and change color; ch 3, turn.

Row 86: Make first shell *bet first and second shell* of row below; make 83 more shells across row to include shell in top of turning ch, change color; ch 3, turn.

Rep rows 85 and 86 for 12 inches—each row contains 84 shells.

Next row: Make first shell bet first and second shell of row, make 82 more shells across, dc in top of turning ch; ch 3, turn—83 shells across. Rep last row, making 1 less shell than in previous row. Continue until 1 shell rem; fasten off.

BORDER: Work 1 rnd of each of 9 colors used in afghan. Join any color in any corner; **ch 3, in same place as join, work 2 dc, ch 3, 3 dc—beg corner made.** Work 3-dc shells evenly spaced around entire afghan, adjusting so work lies flat. Work (3 dc, ch 3, 3 dc) in each corner stitch; join with sl st to top of ch-3 at beg of rnd; fasten off.

Next rnd: Join new color in ch-3 sp of corner and work beg corner. Work 3 dc shells bet each shell-grp around, working 3 dc, ch 3, 3 dc in ch-3 corner lp.

Rep last rnd 6 times more.

Last rnd–picot edging: Join yarn in first dc of any shell group, ch 1, sc in same st as join; *** ch 3, sl st to sc just made—picot made;** sc in next 2 dc, make picot, sc in sp bet shell-grp, sc in next dc. Rep from * around; join to first sc; fasten off.

Striped Crocheted Afghan

Shown on page 7.

Finished size is 44x63 inches, excluding fringe.

MATERIALS
Brunswick Germantown knitting worsted (220-yard skeins): 2 skeins *each* of No. 4021 light azalea, No. 469 horizon blue, No. 400 white, No. 40154 pale terra cotta, No. 440 jade, No. 4361 ocher, No. 4020 light mulberry, No. 416 light spruce, and No. 4123 light copenhagen blue
Size G aluminum crochet hook, or size to obtain gauge given below

Abbreviations: See page 73.
Gauge: In pat st, two 2-dc grps = 1 inch.

INSTRUCTIONS
The afghan is worked in the following 2-row color sequence: light azalea, horizon blue, white, pale terra cotta, jade, ocher, light mulberry, light spruce, light copenhagen blue. Rep the color sequence 7 times more, ending with 2 rows of light azalea.

With light azalea, ch 160.
Row 1: Dc in third ch from hook, ch 3, sc around the post from *front* of beg ch-3 lp, *** dc in each of next 2 ch—2-dc grp made;** ch 3, sc around post from *front* of first dc of 2-dc grp just made; rep from * across, ch 2, turn.

Row 2: Work 2 sc in *each* ch-3 lp across. Make color change in last sc at end of row as follows: **work sc until 2 lps rem on hook, drop color in use, with new color, yo, draw through 2 lps on hook;** then ch 3, turn.

Row 3: Sk first sc, dc in next sc, ch 3, sc around the post from *front* of beg ch-3 of row, * dc in each of next 2 sc, ch 3, sc around post from *front* of first dc of 2-dc grp just made; rep from * across; ch 2, turn.

Row 4: Rep Row 2.

Rep rows 3 and 4, working 2 rows of each color as described above, ending with Row 2 using light azalea; fasten off.

FRINGE: Fold and knot three 6-inch strands of yarn into every other st cross the short sides of the afghan.

Knitted Striped Afghan

Shown on pages 8 and 9.

Finished size is 50x60 inches, excluding fringe.

MATERIALS
For knitting the afghan
Brunswick Germantown knitting worsted (220-yard skeins): 1 skein *each* of No. 400 white, No. 4021 light azalea, No. 4123 light copenhagen blue, No. 4121 copenhagen blue, and No. 445 medium green

2 skeins *each* of No. 467 jade heather, No. 2415 pink heather, No. 2464 pewter heather, No. 4031 medium yellow, and No. 2406 orange

22-inch circular knitting needle, Size 7 or size to obtain gauge given below

For the duplicate-stitch embroidery

Scraps of No. 412 royal blue, No. 4151 calypso pink, No. 4051 saffron, and No. 446 forest green

Blunt-end tapestry needle

Abbreviations: See page 77.
Gauge: 4 sts = 1 inch; 6 rows = 1 inch.

INSTRUCTIONS

Note: The entire afghan is worked in stockinette stitch (k 1 row, p 1 row). The vertical stripes are worked in duplicate stitches when afghan is completed. Work in color sequence of your choice or follow directions below for horizontal striping in afghan shown on pages 8 and 9.

With jade heather, cast on 200 sts and work 2 rows; end off. Continuing in st st, and ending off each color after it is worked, work color sequence as follows: 6 rows with black, 1 row with white, 1 row with pewter heather, * 8 rows with jade heather, 2 rows with pewter heather, 10 rows with copenhagen blue, 2 rows with pewter heather, 8 rows with light copenhagen blue, 2 rows with pewter heather, 14 rows with orange, 2 rows with pewter heather, 18 rows with medium yellow, 2 rows with pewter heather, 6 rows with light azalea, 2 rows with pewter heather, 16 rows with pink heather, 2 rows with pewter heather, 6 rows with black, 1 row with white, 1 row with pewter heather, 10 rows with medium green, 2 rows with pewter heather; rep from * 2 times more, *except* on the second rep, work only until 6 rows of black are completed. End with 2 rows of jade green; bind off. Work in ends on wrong side and block.

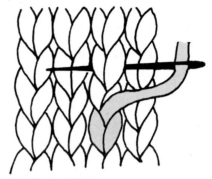

Duplicate Stitch

DUPLICATE-STITCH EMBROIDERY: Work duplicate stitches over 2 knitted sts and over 2 rows using 2 strands of yarn.

With the right side facing, begin at bottom edge on right corner of afghan and work toward left side. Sk first 12 sts from next side edge, work duplicate st over 2 sts with calypso pink; sk 2 sts, work duplicate st with forest green; sk 26 sts, work duplicate st with royal blue; sk 2 sts, work duplicate st with medium yellow; sk 8 sts, work duplicate st with saffron; sk 26 sts, work duplicate st with calypso pink; sk 6 sts, work duplicate st with pewter heather; sk 16 sts, work duplicate st with calypso pink; sk 26 sts, work duplicate st with saffron; sk 8 sts, work duplicate st with medium yellow; sk 2 sts, work duplicate st with royal blue; sk 26 sts, work duplicate st with forest green; sk 2 sts, work duplicate st with calypso pink.

FINISHING: With jade heather, work 1 row sc evenly spaced around entire afghan, working 3 sc in each corner.

Cut 10-inch lengths of yarn from all colors of yarn. In bundles of 7 strands, knot fringe to both short ends. Block to complete.

Puff–Stitch Crocheted Afghan

Shown on page 10.

Finished size is 51x73 inches, including border.

MATERIALS

Unger Roly Poly acrylic worsted-weight yarn (3½-ounce balls): 1 skein *each* of No. 9263 light gray, No. 9512 dark gray, No. 8841 ecru, No. 9216 beige, No. 8767 black, No. 9124 dark brown, No. 8468 maroon, No. 6674 colonial blue, No. 7090 dark blue, No. 9123 dark green, No. 6673 olive green, No. 8322 dark rose, No. 11223 light rose, No. 8310 salmon, No. 8550 peach, and No. 1015 turquoise

2 skeins of No. 864 red

Size F aluminum crochet hook, or size to obtain gauge given below

Abbreviations: See page 73.
Gauge: One square = 5⅜x5⅜ inches.

INSTRUCTIONS

Make a total of 117 squares. Each square is made of 6 rounds. Begin with light color and work each successive rnd in a darker or contrasting color.

Beginning at center, ch 6, join with sl st to form ring.

Rnd 1: Ch 1, work 12 sc in ring; join with sl st to first sc.

Rnd 2: Ch 1, sc in same st as join; (ch 1, sc in next sc) 11 times; ch 1, join with sl st to first sc at beg of rnd—12 ch-1 sps.

Rnd 3: Sl st into first ch-1 sp; **ch 3, drawing up lps to measure ½ inch, (yo, draw up lp in same ch-1 sp) twice; yo, draw through 5 lps on hook—beg puff st made.** Ch 2, * in next ch-1 sp make puff st as follows: **(yo, draw up loop) 3 times, yo, draw through 7 loops on hook—puff st made;** ch 2, rep

continued

SCRAP-SAVER DESIGNS

from * around—12 puff sts made; ch 2, join with sl st to top of ch-3 at beg of rnd; fasten off.

Rnd 4: Attach new color in any ch-2 sp and work a beg puff st. * (Ch 2, work puff st in next ch-2 sp) twice, ch 3 for corner, puff st in next ch-2 sp; rep from * twice; end (ch 2, puff st in next ch-2 sp) twice, ch 3, join with sl st to top of ch-3 at beg of rnd; fasten off.

Rnd 5: Attach new color in any ch-3 corner sp and work a beg puff st, ch 3, puff st in same corner sp; * (ch 2, puff st in next ch-2 sp) twice; ch 2, in corner ch-3 sp work (puff st, ch 3, puff st). Rep from * twice; end (ch 2, puff st in ch-2 sp) twice, ch 2, join with sl st to top of ch-3 at beg of rnd—16 puff sts made; fasten off.

Rnd 6: Attach new color in any ch-3 corner sp. Ch 3, in same sp, work 2 dc, ch 2, 3 dc, * ch 1, (in next ch-2 sp work 3 dc, ch 1) 3 times, in ch-3 corner sp work 3 dc, ch 2, 3 dc). Rep from * 3 times; end ch 1, sl st to top of ch-3 at beg of rnd; fasten off.

ASSEMBLY: With right sides tog and working in the *back lps,* whipstitch the squares tog. Make 9 strips with 13 squares in each strip. Sew strips tog.

BORDER: Using colors of your choice, work as follows: Work 2 rnds of sc around entire afghan with 1 color, working 3 sc in each corner so work lies flat; join to first sc; fasten off.

Rnd 3: Join next color and work as for first 2 rnds; fasten off.

Next rnd: Working with 2 colors, work 3 sc of each color alternately around. (Carry the unused color under the 3-sc group of the color in use.) Continue in the 3-sc pattern around the entire afghan to the starting point; *do not join;* mark last st in rnd.

Next rnd: Rep the previous rnd, working the same color above each 3-sc group in the previous rnd. Join to marked sc; fasten off.

Next rnd: Attach new color in any sc, ch 1, and work sc in each sc around; join, fasten off.

Next 2 rnds: Join any color in any sc, ch 1, and sc in each sc around; do not join, mark last sc; sc in each sc around; join to marked sc; fasten off.

Last rnd–picot edging: Attach new color in any sc; * work 1 sc in each of next 2 sts, ch 3, sl st in sc just made. Rep from * around; fasten off.

Granny Square Doll Blanket

Shown on page 11.

Finished size is 22½x29½ inches, including border.

MATERIALS
Unger Roly Sport yarn (1¾-ounce balls), 3 balls of black
Scraps of various colors of yarn (the equivalent of approximately 3 balls)
Size F aluminum crochet hook, or size to obtain gauge

Knitting and Crocheting with Bobbins

If you've never worked with bobbins, you may want to try them the next time you're knitting or crocheting a multicolored pattern. Changing colors is simpler when you stitch with bobbins because you no longer need to carry an entire ball of yarn for every color in the design. Here are some tips to help you work successfully with bobbins.

Bobbins generally are available in two sizes. Use the smaller size for baby, fingering, sock, and other lightweight yarns. Use the larger size for sport, worsted, or bulky yarns.

To determine how much yarn to wind on a bobbin, estimate the width of the area you plan to stitch in a color. Cut yarn for the bobbin four times longer than your estimate.

Use a separate bobbin for each color, except the main color, in the design you are stitching.

To fill the bobbin, wrap the yarn *horizontally* around the bobbin three times, and then wrap it *vertically* once to fasten it in the slot. Continue winding in this way until you've wound all the yarn or filled the bobbin.

Avoid overloading the bobbin. It is better to wind and tie in another bobbin at a convenient point in your work than to wrap it too tightly or too full. Join the new bobbin at a point where colors change or at a place where joining will not be obvious.

When knitting, as you work across the row and come to your next color, drop the color in use on the side the stitch ends (knits at back of work, purls at front of work). With the right hand, pick up the new color from *beneath* the old one and work the next stitch. Bringing the new yarn *under* the old yarn twists the yarns together and makes a loop that prevents a hole where the two colors join.

Maintain your regular working tension when changing colors between the stitches; do not pull these stitches tightly.

When crocheting, work up to the stitch before the color change, then work the next stitch to the point where there are two loops on the hook. Drop the color in use and with the next color, wrap the yarn over the hook (yo) and draw the yarn through the remaining two loops on the hook. Always drop the last bobbin used to the front side as the work faces you.

A word of caution: As convenient as they are, bobbins can only be used when you are knitting or crocheting in *rows.* You cannot work in *rounds* with bobbins because at the end of a round the bobbin will be at the *end* of the color area (rather than the beginning) when you start the next round of stitches.

Abbreviations: See page 73.
Gauge: One square measures 2½x2½ inches.

INSTRUCTIONS

GRANNY SQUARE (make 63): With any color, ch 4, join to form ring. *Rnd 1:* Ch 3, 2 dc in ring, ch 1, (3 dc in ring, ch 1) 3 times; join to top of ch-3; fasten off.

Rnd 2: Join second color in any ch-1 sp; **ch 3, in same sp work 2 dc, ch 1, 3 dc—first corner made;** (ch 1, in next ch-1 sp work 3 dc, ch 1, 3 dc) 3 times; ch 1, join to top of ch-3; fasten off.

Rnd 3: Join black in any ch-1 corner sp and work a first corner, (ch 1, 3 dc in next ch-1 sp, in next ch-1 corner sp work 3 dc, ch 1, 3 dc) 3 times; ch 1, 3 dc in next ch-1 sp, ch 1, join; fasten off.

ASSEMBLY: Make 9 strips with 7 squares in each strip. Whip-stitch squares tog with black yarn.

BORDER: Attach blue yarn in any corner ch-sp, ch 3, in same sp work 2 dc, ch 1, 2 trc, ch 1, and 3 dc. * Ch 1, in next sp work 2 dc, ch 1, trc, ch 1, 2 dc. Rep from * to next corner sp; in corner sp work 3 dc, ch 1, 2 trc, ch 1, 3 dc. Work rem 3 sides to correspond; end ch 1, join to top of ch-3; fasten off.

Knitted Fair Isle Afghan

Shown on pages 12 and 13.

Finished size is approximately 48x60 inches.

MATERIALS

Bucilla Softex (4-ounce balls): 1 ball *each* of colors A (off-white), B (rose), and C (navy)
Bucilla Softex Spectrum Shades (3-ounce balls): 1 ball *each* of colors D (dark brown), E (light brown), F (light red), G (medium red), H (light blue), J (medium blue), and K (rust)
Size 6 knitting needles
Size G crochet hook

Abbreviations: See page 73.
Gauge: Working in stockinette stitch, 5 sts = 1 inch; 7 rows = 1 inch.

INSTRUCTIONS

The afghan contains 80 squares. For all squares, cast on 31 sts and work in st st (k 1 row, p 1 row) for 42 rows. Bind off.

SOLID-COLOR SQUARE: Follow the instructions for the square above, using colors of your choice.

STRIPED SQUARE: Cast on 31 sts and work 1 row with first color, * work 4 rows with second color, then work 4 rows with first color; rep from * 4 times more, work 1 row with second color. Bind off with second color.

PATTERNED SQUARE: Work motif patterns in duplicate st (see diagram, page 17) when square is completed, or work design as you knit the square. When knitting in, use a separate 2-yard strand of each color for each motif. When picking up next color, always bring color to be used from *under* color last used. Carry yarn not in use loosely across wrong side, twisting with working strand every third stitch.

Make patterned squares alike, as charted, or work as we did, making each square different by changing the number and position of motifs.

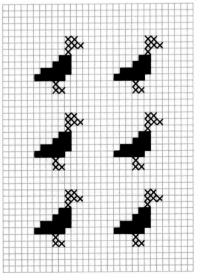

1 Square = 1 Stitch

1 Square = 1 Stitch

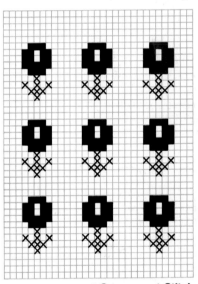

1 Square = 1 Stitch

FINISHING: Using the colors of your choice, whipstitch all the squares tog as desired.

EDGING: With Size G crochet hook and right side facing, join yarn in any corner; work 3 sc in same corner st, sc evenly spaced around outside edge of afghan and continue to work 3 sc in each corner st; join to first sc.

Rnd 2: Ch 1, sc in same st as join, work 3 sc in each corner sc, sc in each sc around, join to first sc. Rep Rnd 2 twice more; fasten off. Block to complete.

PATCHWORK PATTERNS

FOR AFGHANS AND THROWS

Few forms of American folk art have inspired as many new craft designs as have traditional patchwork motifs. This chapter contains eight intriguing variations on a patchwork theme, from Log Cabin strip-piecing to floral appliqué adaptations. In addition to their crocheted or knitted patterns, these afghans make the most of appealing changes in texture—also characteristic of fine hand quilting.

This exquisite design derives from the Flying Geese pattern, long a favorite of America's quilters.

The finished afghan measures 60 inches square, but it is stitched in nine separate panels varying in size from 5 to 7½ inches wide. You can work the individual panels quickly. And because the design is stitched in strips, you can carry this project easily wherever you go, to work on it in brief moments between your other activities.

The four motif panels (each 7½ inches wide) feature knitted-in triangles worked in moss stitch on a stockinette-stitch background. Yarn bobbins simplify changing colors on these panels. (See page 18 for tips and techniques for knitting or crocheting with bobbins.)

The remaining end and center panels (5 and 6 inches wide) are worked in stockinette- and reverse stockinette-stitch triangles. Textured panels such as these call to mind the elaborately quilted sashing strips and borders found on many patchwork quilts.

How-to instructions for all of the afghans in this chapter begin on page 32.

PATCHWORK PATTERNS

Log Cabin designs are among patchworkers' favorite patterns. And no wonder! Once pieced, the blocks can be set together in an almost infinite number of ways.

Blocks in this 53x61-inch afghan and the companion pillows are assembled in three of the most popular Log Cabin sets—the Straight Furrow design (on the afghan and the pillow in the foreground), the Barn Raising pattern (on the pillow, *left*), and the Courthouse Steps design (on the pillow in the background, *right*).

Each of the 6¼-inch-square blocks features a characteristic red center, symbolic of the hearth or heart of the cabin. Surrounding the center are light and dark double crochet "logs."

In the blocks used for the Straight Furrow and Barn Raising patterns, logs in related colors are adjacent to one another, making one half of each block light and the other half dark. In the Courthouse Steps blocks, logs in similar shades are on opposing sides.

PATCHWORK PATTERNS

Beloved for their dignified but dramatic color schemes and often elegant quilting, Amish quilts are an endless source of inspiration for afghans. When stitching these patterns, knitters and crocheters can indulge their fancy for textured stitches to simulate the elaborate quilting patterns found on antique Amish coverlets.

The crocheted afghan, *opposite*, is patterned after the Square-in-Square design. Begun with a center square, this 42x42-inch design makes use of various texture stitches with each color change.

The traditional Irish Chain design translates beautifully into the knitted 54-inch-square afghan, *above*.

Simply made with stockinette stitches and a garter-stitch border, this two-color design is stitched in a single piece. It relies on an orderly progression of color changes to create the alternating blue and white squares. Using yarn bobbins keeps the work flat.

PATCHWORK PATTERNS

Once you can stitch a perfect square, you'll find dozens of quilt designs suitable for crochet—the number of patchwork patterns pieced from squares is almost limitless. Armed with graph paper, colored pencils, and your own imagination, you can create an entire collection of patchwork-style afghans, throws, and coverlets.

You might begin by stitching this 54x73-inch throw adapted from a traditional Chimney Sweep design.

Each of the 6¼-inch-square blocks features four groups of treble crochet stitches worked around a center ring. Successive rounds of treble crochet groups are stitched into the tops of the previous groups and at right angles to them.

A final round of single, half-double, and double crochet stitches straightens the sides of the squares. Stitch 85 complete blocks and 24 half-blocks in two color schemes for the complete design.

Then, to finish the afghan, assemble the squares and half-squares just as patchworkers assemble a quilt pieced in squares and half-squares: Arrange the blocks in diagonal rows, fill the edges with half-blocks, and border the design with a treble crochet "binding."

PATCHWORK PATTERNS

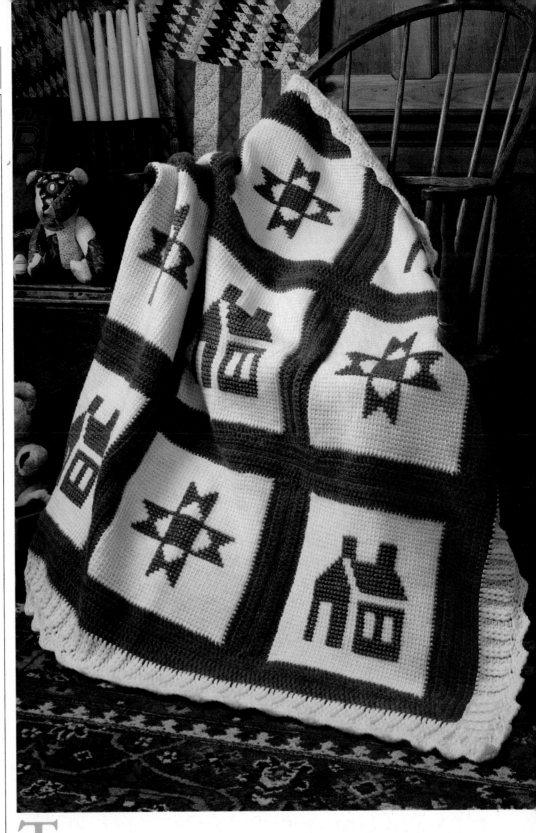

orking cross-stitch motifs atop afghan-stitch panels is an easy way to imitate appliqué or intricately pieced patchwork motifs.

The rose-patterned afghan, *opposite*, features a single motif repeated along the length of each panel. The roses in adjacent panels are offset to form the overall design. Rows of twining, Victorian-style ribbons define the edges of the panels. Real ribbons are woven through the lacy mesh border of this 58x70-inch coverlet.

The familiar Schoolhouse and Ohio Star patterns appear on the square afghan, *above.* These motifs are embroidered atop afghan-stitch squares worked in single colors; the colors reappear in the lovely crocheted border. This design measures 45x45 inches.

Afghan-stitch panels, which are limited in width by the length of the afghan hook, can be worked either in long strips such as for the rose-pattern design, or in blocks as for the Schoolhouse design.

PATCHWORK PATTERNS

This lively afghan has all the features of a Victorian crazy quilt— playful and sentimental designs, seemingly haphazard placement of motifs, and touches of embroidery to outline individual blocks.

Knit this 39x39-inch throw in six panels. To avoid having to join individual squares into rows, just change the yarn color after each square is complete and continue knitting to the end of the panel.

Then, after the panels are knitted, add the motifs with duplicate-stitch embroidery. Our embroidered squares include tulip and thistle motifs and bow, dog, butterfly, and fruit motifs. (You'll find two color schemes noted in the color keys accompanying the designs. Use the first set of colors for one motif, and the second set for another motif.) Use scraps of three-ply Persian yarn for this step.

Leave the panels plain, or accent each square with embroidery stitches—the more varied the better— around each square. A single crochet border and tassel-style fringe complete the afghan.

PATCHWORK PATTERNS

Flying Geese Afghan

Shown on pages 20 and 21.

Finished size is 60x60 inches.

MATERIALS
Bernat Berella 4 knitting worsted (100-gram balls): 9 balls of No. 8941 ecru and 2 balls *each* of No. 8886 light gold, No. 8955 copper, No. 8924 bois de rose, No. 8864 dark green, and No. 8866 light green
Size 8 knitting needles
Set of knitting bobbins

Abbreviations: See page 77.
Gauge: 4 sts = 1 inch; 5 rows = 1 inch.

INSTRUCTIONS:
Afghan is worked in 9 panels.

CENTER CHECKERED PANELS (make 3): Cast on 20 sts. Work in garter stitch (k every row) for 12 rows for border.
Row 1: K 3, (p 6, k 1) 2 times; k 3.
Row 2: K 3, (p 2, k 5) 2 times; k 3.
Row 3: K 3, (p 4, k 3) 2 times; k 3.
Row 4: K 3, (p 4, k 3) 2 times; k 3.
Row 5: K 3, (p 2, k 5) 2 times; k 3.
Row 6: K 3, (p 6, k 1) 2 times; k 3.
Row 7: K all stitches.
Row 8: K 3, (k 6, p 1) 2 times; k 3.
Row 9: K 3, (k 2, p 5) 2 times; k 3.
Row 10: K 3, (k 4, p 3) 2 times; k 3.
Row 11: K 3, (k 4, p 3) 2 times; k 3.
Row 12: K 3, (k 2, p 5) 2 times; k 3.
Row 13: K 3, (k 6, p 1) 2 times; k 3.
Row 14: K 3, p 14, k 3.
Rep rows 1–14 twenty-four times more. Work 12 rows of garter stitch; bind off.

RIGHT BORDER CHECKERED PANEL (make 1): Cast on 24 sts. Work in garter stitch for 12 rows.
Row 1: K 7, (p 6, k 1) 2 times; k 3.
Row 2: K 3, (p 2, k 5) 2 times; k 7.
Row 3: K 7, (p 4, k 3) 2 times; k 3.
Row 4: K 3, (p 4, k 3) 2 times; k 7.
Row 5: K 7, (p 2, k 5) 2 times; k 3.
Row 6: K 3, (p 6, k 1) 2 times; k 7.
Row 7: K all stitches.
Row 8: K 3, (k 6, p 1) 2 times; k 7.
Row 9: K 7, (k 2, p 5) 2 times; k 3.
Row 10: K 3, (k 4, p 3) 2 times; k 7.
Row 11: K 7, (k 4, p 3) 2 times; k 3.
Row 12: K 3, (k 2, p 5) 2 times; k 7.
Row 13: K 7, (k 6, p 1) 2 times; k 3.
Row 14: K 3, p 14, k 7.
Rep rows 1–14 twenty-four times more. Work 12 rows of garter stitch; bind off.

LEFT BORDER CHECKERED PANEL (make 1): Cast on 24 sts. Work in garter stitch for 12 rows.
Row 1: K 3, (p 6, k 1) 2 times; k 7.
Row 2: K 7, (p 2, k 5) 2 times; k 3.
Row 3: K 3, (p 4, k 3) 2 times; k 7.
Row 4: K 7, (p 4, k 3) 2 times; k 3.
Row 5: K 3, (p 2, k 5) 2 times; k 7.
Row 6: K 7, (p 6, k 1) 2 times; k 3.
Row 7: K all stitches.
Row 8: K 7, (k 6, p 1) 2 times; k 3.
Row 9: K 3, (k 2, p 5) 2 times; k 7.
Row 10: K 7, (k 4, p 3) 2 times; k 3.
Row 11: K 3, (k 4, p 3) 2 times; k 7.
Row 12: K 7, (k 2, p 5) 2 times; k 3.
Row 13: K 3, (k 6, p 1) 2 times; k 7.
Row 14: K 7, p 14, k 3.

Rep rows 1–14 twenty-four times more. Work 12 rows of garter stitch; bind off.

FLYING GEESE PANEL (make 4): Change color as desired for each triangle as you work. When changing color, twist yarn as you begin with new color and *always* leave bobbin just worked on the *wrong* (purl) side of work.
Before beginning, wind 3 bobbins, 2 with ecru and 1 with color of triangle.
With ecru, cast on 31 stitches; work 12 rows of garter stitch. Beg pat st working with bobbins.
Row 1: With ecru, k 3, change to color bobbin, and work (p 1, k 1) 12 times; p 1; change to ecru, k 3.
Row 2: With ecru, k 4; with color, (p 1, k 1) 11 times; p 1, change to ecru, k 4.
Row 3: With ecru, k 3, p 2; with color, (k 1, p 1) 10 times; k 1; with ecru, p 2, k 3.
Row 4: With ecru, k 6; with color, (k 1, p 1) 9 times, k 1; with ecru, k 6.
Row 5: With ecru, k 3, p 4; with color, (p 1, k 1) 8 times, p 1; with ecru, p 4, k 3.
Row 6: With ecru, k 8; with color, (p 1, k 1) 7 times, p 1; with ecru, k 8.
Row 7: With ecru, k 3, p 6; with color, (k 1, p 1) 6 times, k 1; with ecru, p 6, k 3.
Row 8: With ecru, k 10; with color, (k 1, p 1) 5 times, k 1; with ecru, k 10.
Row 9: With ecru, k 3, p 8; with color, (p 1, k 1) 4 times, p 1; with ecru, p 8, k 3.
Row 10: With ecru, k 12; with color, (p 1, k 1) 3 times, p 1; with ecru, k 12.
Row 11: With ecru, k 3, p 10; with color, (k 1, p 1) twice, k 1; with ecru, p 10, k 3.
Row 12: With ecru, k 14; with color, k 1, p 1, k 1; with ecru, k 14.
Row 13: With ecru, k 3, p 12; with color, p 1; with ecru, p 12, k 3.
Row 14: With ecru, k across the row. Tie off color bobbin. Rep rows 1–14 twenty-four times more, changing color of each triangle. Work 12 rows of garter stitch with ecru; bind off.

FINISHING: Whipstitch panels together, placing checkered panel between each triangular panel and placing border checkered panels on correct sides.

Log Cabin Crocheted Afghan

Shown on pages 22 and 23.

Finished size is 53x61 inches, including border.

MATERIALS
Anny Blatt No. 4 "Sport" (1¾-ounce skeins): 4 skeins *each* of No. 1287 cerise, No. 1875 zinc, and No. 1881 sapin
1 skein *each* of No. 1882 framboisine and No. 1560 prusse
2 skeins *each* of No. 1298 ecru, No. 1300 havane, No. 1301 grège, No. 1294 perle, No. 1295 souris, No. 1296 acier, No. 1283 paille, No. 1284 rose, No. 1871 saumon, No. 1880 cognac, 1566 cuivré, and No. 1569 mûre
Size F aluminum crochet hook

Abbreviations: See page 73.
Gauge: One square measures 6¼x6¼ inches.

INSTRUCTIONS
For the light and dark blocks
These blocks are used for the Straight Furrow afghan and the Barn Raising pillow. See pages 34 and 35.

Note: All dcs are worked on *right* side of work; all ch-3 lps are worked on *wrong* side of work.

CENTER SQUARE: With cerise, ch 5, join with sl st to form ring.
Rnd 1 (right side): Ch 3, 2 dc in ring, (ch 1, 3 dc in ring) 3 times; ch 1, join with sl st to top of ch-3 at beg of rnd, turn.
Rnd 2: **In first ch-1 sp, work sc, ch 3, sc—corner made;** * ch 3, **in next ch-1 sp work sc, ch 3, sc—another corner made;** rep from * 2 times more; ch 3, sl st in sc at beg of rnd; turn.

Rnd 3: Sl st into first ch-3 lp; ch 3, 2 dc in same lp, * in next ch-3 corner-lp work 3 dc, ch 1, 3 dc; 3 dc in next ch-3 lp, rep from * 2 times more; end 3 dc, ch 1, 3 dc in last ch-3 corner lp. Join with sl st to top of ch-3; fasten off.

FIRST COLOR BAND: With *wrong* side facing, join a *light-color* yarn in any ch-1 corner sp, (ch 3, sl st in sp bet next two 3-dc grps) twice; ch 3, sl st in ch-1 corner sp; turn.
Sl st into ch-3 lp, ch 3, 2 dc in same lp, (3 dc in next ch-3 lp) twice; ch 3, turn. (Sl st in sp between next two 3-dc grps, ch 3) twice, sl st in top of turning ch-3, turn.
Sl st into ch-3 lp; ch 3, 2 dc in same lp, (3 dc in next ch-3 lp) twice; fasten off.

SECOND COLOR BAND: With *wrong* side facing, join a second *light-color* yarn in top of ch-3 at *beg* of *last row,* ch 3, sl st in sp bet next 2 rows of dcs, ch 3, sl st in *ch-1 corner sp of center square;* (ch 3, sl st bet next 2 dc-grps) twice, ch 3, sl st in ch-1 corner-sp; turn.
Sl st into ch-3 lp, ch 3, 2 dc in same lp, (3 dc in next ch-3 lp) 4 times; ch 3, turn.
(Sl st in sp bet next 2 dc-grps, ch 3) 4 times; sl st in top of turning ch-3, turn. Sl st into ch-3 lp, ch 3, 2 dc in same lp, (3 dc in next ch-3 lp) 4 times; fasten off.

THIRD COLOR BAND: With *wrong* side facing, join a *dark-color* yarn in top of ch-3 at *beg of last row.* Ch 3, sl st in sp bet next 2 rows of dcs, ch 3, sl st in *ch-1 corner sp of center square,* (ch 3, sl st bet next 2 dc-grps) twice. Ch 3, sl st in ch-1 corner sp; turn.
Sl st into ch-3 lp, ch 3, 2 dc in same lp; (3 dc in next ch-3 lp) 4 times, ch 3, turn.
Sl st in sp bet next 2 dc-grps; (ch 3, sl st in sp bet next 2 dc-grps) 3 times, ch 3, sl st in top of turning ch-3, turn.
Sl st into ch-3 lp, ch 3, 2 dc in same lp; (3 dc in next ch-3 lp) 4 times; fasten off.

FOURTH COLOR BAND: With *wrong* side facing, join a *dark-color* yarn in top of ch-3 at *beg of last row.* Ch 3, sl st in sp bet next 2 rows of dcs, ch 3, sl st in ch-1 corner sp of center square, (ch 3, sl st bet next 2 dc-grps) twice, ch 3, sl st in ch-1 corner-sp of center square, ch 3, sl st bet next 2 rows of dcs, ch 3, sl st in dc of first color band; turn.
Sl st into ch-3 lp, ch 3, 2 dc in same lp; (3 dc in next ch-3 lp) 6 times; ch 3, turn.
Sl st in sp bet next 2 dc-grps; (ch 3, sl st in sp bet next 2 dc-grps) 5 times; ch 3, sl st in top of turning ch-3, turn.
Sl st into ch-3 lp, ch 3, 2 dc in same lp; (3 dc in next ch-3 lp) 6 times; fasten off.

FIFTH COLOR BAND: With *wrong* side facing, join a *light-color* yarn in top of ch-3 at *beg of last row.* (Ch 3, sl st in sp bet next 2 rows of dcs) twice, (ch 3, sl st bet next 2 dc-grps) twice, ch 3, sl st bet next 2 rows of dcs, ch 3, sl st in dc of color band; turn.
Sl st into ch-3 lp, ch 3, 2 dc in same lp; (3 dc in next ch-3 lp) 6 times; ch 3, turn.
Sl st in sp bet next 2 dc-grps; (ch 3, sl st in sp bet next 2 dc-grps) 5 times; ch 3, sl st in top of turning ch-3, turn.
Sl st into ch-3 lp, ch 3, 2 dc in same lp; (3 dc in next ch-3 lp) 6 times; fasten off.

SIXTH COLOR BAND: With *wrong* side facing, join a *light-color* yarn in top of ch-3 at *beg of last row.* (Ch 3, sl st in sp bet next 2 rows of dcs) twice, (ch 3, sl st bet next 2 dc-grps) 5 times, ch 3, sl st bet next 2 rows of dcs, ch 3, sl st in dc of color band; turn.
Sl st into ch-3 lp, ch 3, 2 dc in same lp; (3 dc in next ch-3 lp) 8 times; ch 3, turn.
Sl st in sp bet next 2 dc-grps; (ch 3, sl st in sp bet next 2 dc-grps) 7 times; ch 3, sl st in top of turning ch-3, turn.
Sl st into ch-3 lp, ch 3, 2 dc in same lp; (3 dc in next ch-3 lp) 8 times; fasten off.

continued

PATCHWORK PATTERNS

Straight Furrow

SEVENTH AND EIGHTH COLOR BANDS: Work in pat as established, working 2 more *dark* color bands.

Make a total of 72 squares. Referring to diagram, *opposite,* arrange squares in furrows with darks and lights running diagonally across the afghan; whipstitch the blocks tog through the back lps, changing colors for each block and color band as you sew.

BORDER: *Rnd 1:* With wrong side facing, join zinc in top of ch-3 in any corner, in same st work sc, ch 3, sc; * (ch 3, sl st bet next 2 rows of dcs) twice, (ch 3, sl st bet next 2 dc-grps) 8 times, ch 3, sl st in join bet 2 blocks, rep from * to next corner st; in corner st work sc, ch 3, sc. Rep from * around; join last ch-3 with sl st to sc at beg of rnd; turn.

Rnd 2: Sl st into ch-3 lp, ch 3, in same lp work 2 dc; * in next ch-3 lp work 3 dc; rep from * to next corner; work 2 dc, ch 2, 2 dc in ch-3 corner-lp. Rep from first * around; join with sl st to top of ch-3 at beg of rnd.

Rnds 3 and 4: Ch 3, dc in next dc and each dc to corner lp, * in corner lp, work 2 dc, ch 2, 2 dc; dc in each dc to next corner; rep from * around; join with sl st to top of ch-3; fasten off.

Rnds 5–9: Join sapin in corner ch-2 lp; 3 sc in same lp, sc in each st around, working 3 sc in corner lps; do not join; continue in pat as established; join at end of Rnd 9; fasten off.

Rnd 10: Join cerise in any sc, and working *clockwise,* work sc in same sc as join, * ch 1, sk next sc, sc in next sc; rep from * around; join to first sc; fasten off.

For Courthouse Steps block

This block is used for the pillow, *center right.*

Note: All dcs are worked on *right* side of work; all ch-3 lps are worked on *wrong* side of work.

CENTER SQUARE: Work as for Center Square of Barn Raising block, page 33.

FIRST COLOR BAND: Work as for First Color Band of Barn Raising block.

SECOND COLOR BAND: Turn, rotate work, and with another light-color yarn, rep First Color Band on opposite side of block.

THIRD COLOR BAND: With *wrong* side facing, join dark-color yarn in top of ch-3 at beg of last row of last color band worked, ch 3, sl st in sp bet next 2 rows of dcs, ch 3, sl st in *ch-1 corner sp of center square*; (ch 3, sl st bet next 2 dc-grps) twice, ch 3, sl st in ch-1 corner-sp; ch 3, sl st in sp bet next 2 rows of dcs, ch 3, sl st in first dc of next color band; turn.

Sl st into ch-3 lp, ch 3, 2 dc in same lp, (3 dc in next ch-3 lp) 6 times; ch 3, turn.

(Sl st in sp bet next 2 dc-grps, ch 3) 6 times; sl st in top of turning ch-3, turn. Sl st into ch-3 lp, ch 3, 2 dc in same lp, (3 dc in next ch-3 lp) 6 times; fasten off.

FOURTH COLOR BAND: Turn, rotate work, and with another dark-color yarn, join yarn in top of ch-3 at beg of last row of Second Color Band; rep Third Color Band.

FIFTH COLOR BAND: With wrong side facing, join light-color yarn to top of ch-3 at beg of last row of Third Color Band, (ch 3, sl st in sp bet next 2 rows of dcs) twice; (ch 3, sl st bet next 2 dc-grps) 3 times; ch 3, sl st in sp bet next 2 rows of dcs, ch 3, sl st in first dc of next color band; turn.

Sl st into ch-3 lp, ch 3, 2 dc in same lp, (3 dc in next ch-3 lp) 6 times; ch 3, turn.

(Sl st in sp bet next 2 dc-grps, ch 3) 6 times; sl st in top of turning ch-3, turn. Sl st into ch-3 lp, ch 3, 2 dc in same lp, (3 dc in next ch-3 lp) 6 times; fasten off.

SIXTH COLOR BAND: Turn, rotate work, and join another light-color yarn in top of ch-3 at beg of last row of Fourth Color Band; rep Fifth Color Band.

SEVENTH AND EIGHTH COLOR BANDS: Work in pat as established, working 2 more *dark-color* bands.

For the pillows

Work 4 identical blocks for each pillow as established in instructions. Using diagrams, *below,* assemble and work borders as for afghan.

Barn Raising

Courthouse Steps

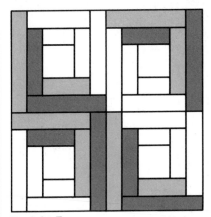

Straight Furrow

Irish Chain Quilt Afghan

Shown on page 25.

Finished size is 55x55 inches.

MATERIALS
Pingouin Pingofrance (150-yard balls): 8 balls of No. 126 azure and 9 balls of No. 153 ecru
22-inch Size 7 circular knitting needle
Set of knitting bobbins

Abbreviations: See page 77.
Gauge: 9 sts = 2 inches; 7 rows = 1 inch.

INSTRUCTIONS
BORDER: With blue, cast on 255 sts. Work in garter st (k every row) for 24 rows.

IRISH CHAIN PATTERN: Before beg, wind 6 bobbins with blue yarn and 3 bobbins with white yarn. Continue to work 15 sts on both ends for borders in garter st and begin to work stockinette st (k right-side row, p wrong-side row) for Irish Chain pattern.
Note: When making color changes, drop the bobbin to the side where the stitch ends and bring the new bobbin *under* the previous bobbin, twisting the new colors to avoid making a hole. (See tip box on page 18.)
Row 1: K 30 blue, k 15 white, k 15 blue; join ball of white yarn, k 45; k 15 blue, k 15 white, k 15 blue; join ball of white yarn, k 45; k 15 blue, k 15 white, k 30 blue.
Row 2: K 15 blue for border; p 15 blue, p 15 white, p 15 blue, p 45 white, p 15 blue, p 15 white, p 15 blue, p 45 white, p 15 blue, p 15 white, p 15 blue; end k 15 blue.
Rep rows 1 and 2 for 21 rows, ending with a k row.
Row 22: Changing bobbins as you work, k 15 blue, p 15 white, p 15 blue, p 75 white, p 15 blue, p 75 white, p 15 blue, p 15 white, k 15 blue.

Row 23: K 15 blue, k 15 white, k 15 blue, k 75 white, k 15 blue, k 75 white, k 15 blue, k 15 white, k 15 blue. Rep rows 22 and 23 until 21 rows are completed, ending with a p row.
Rows 43–63: Rep rows 1 and 2 until 21 rows are completed, ending with a k row.
Row 64: K 15 blue, p 45 white, p 15 blue, p 15 white, p 15 blue, p 45 white, p 15 blue, p 15 white, p 15 blue, p 45 white, k 15 blue.
Row 65: K 15 blue, k 45 white, k 15 blue, k 15 white, k 15 blue, k 45 white, k 15 blue, k 15 white, k 15 blue, k 45 white, k 15 blue. Rep rows 64 and 65 until 21 rows are completed, ending with a p row.
Row 85: K 15 blue, k 60 white, k 15 blue, k 75 white, k 15 blue, k 60 white, k 15 blue.
Row 86: K 15 blue, p 60 white, p 15 blue, p 75 white, p 15 blue, p 60 white, k 15 blue. Rep rows 85 and 86 until 21 rows are completed, ending with a k row.
Rows 106–126: Rep rows 64 and 65 until 21 rows are completed, ending with a p row.
Rep rows 1–126.
Rep rows 1–63.
Work garter st border with blue for 24 rows; bind off.

Crocheted Amish Afghan

Shown on page 24.

Finished size is 42 inches square.

MATERIALS
Brunswick knitting worsted (220-yard skeins): 3 skeins of No. 90023 damson; 2 skeins *each* of No. 9060 black and No. 90811 blue velvet; and 1 skein *each* of No. 9085 earth green and No. 9037 raspberry
Size H aluminum crochet hook

Abbreviations: See page 73.
Gauge: 7 sc = 2 inches.

INSTRUCTIONS
CENTER SQUARE: Beg at center, with blue, ch 5; join with sl st to form ring.

Rnd 1: Work 12 sc in ring; mark last sc for end of rnd; do not join.
Rnd 2: Working in *back loops* until specified otherwise, sc in next sc; * 3 sc in next sc—corner made; sc in each of next 2 sc; rep from * 2 times more; end 3 sc in next sc, sc in last sc—20 sc made.
Rnd 3: Moving marker at the end of each rnd, sc in each of next 2 sc; * 3 sc in next sc, sc in each of next 4 sc; rep from * 2 times more; ending 3 sc in next sc, sc in last 2 sc—28 sc made.
Rnd 4: Sc in each of next 3 sc; * 3 sc in next sc, sc in each of next 6 sc; rep from * 2 times more; ending 3 sc in next sc, sc in next 3 sc—36 sc made.
Rnd 5: Sc in each of next 4 sc; * 3 sc in next sc, sc in each of next 8 sc; rep from * 2 times more; ending 3 sc in next sc, sc in each of next 4 sc—44 sc made.
Continue around piece in this manner until 40 sc from corner to corner are made. Work should measure approximately 11 inches square.

BORDER: *Row 1:* Working under both lps, with wrong side facing, join raspberry in center sc of any corner, ch 3, dc in each sc across row; ending dc in center sc of next corner—40 dc, counting beg ch-3 as dc; ch 3, turn.
Row 2: Sk first dc, dc around post of next dc from *front;* * dc around post of each of next 2 dc from *back,* dc around post of each of next 2 dc from *front;* rep from * across row, working last dc in top of turning ch; ch 2, turn.
Row 3: Sk first dc, dc around post of next dc from *back;* * dc around post of each of next 2 dc from *front,* dc around post of each of next 2 dc from *back;* rep from * across row, working last dc in top of turning ch; ch 2, turn.
Rows 4–7: Repeat rows 2 and 3 alternately.
Row 8: Rep Row 2. Fasten off. Rep Border instructions on rem 3 sides.

CORNER BLOCKS: *Row 1:* With right side facing, join earth green around turning ch (dc) at outside edge of any raspberry strip, ch 1, sc in same st as join; * ch 1, sk ¼ inch on raspberry strip, sc around turning ch-lp; rep from * 6 times more—8 sc in row; ch 1, turn.

Row 2: Sc in first sc, sc in next ch-1 sp; * ch 1, sk next sc, sc in next ch-1 sp; rep from * to last sc; sc in last sc; ch 1, turn.

Row 3: Sc in first sc; * ch 1, sk next sc, sc in next ch-1 sp; rep from * to last 2 sc; ch 1, sk next sc, sc in last sc; ch 1, turn.

Rep rows 2 and 3 until length equals length of raspberry strip, ending at inside edge; fasten off, leaving 12-inch strand of yarn, and whipstitch to adjoining raspberry strip.

Rep Corner Block for remaining 3 corners.

TRIANGULAR SECTIONS: Join black, with right side facing, in corner st of any green corner block.

Row 1: Ch 3, sk 2 sts, **3 dc in next st—shell made;** work 21 more shells evenly spaced across row, ending with dc in last st at corner of next green block—22 shells made; ch 3, turn.

Row 2: (Shell in sp bet next 2 shells) 21 times; dc in sp bet last shell and turning-ch; ch 3, turn.

Rows 3–22: Rep Row 2—there will be 1 less shell on each row and 1 shell at end of Row 22; do not ch 3 to turn at end of Row 22; fasten off.

Rep triangular sections on rem 3 sides. Block work at this point if necessary. Lay finished piece on a flat surface and cover with wet towel; allow to dry completely.

BLUE BORDER: *Rnd 1:* With right side facing, join blue in center st of any corner; ch 1, 3 sc in same corner st; * in each turning ch-lp work 2 sc to next corner, sk first dc in corner 3-dc grp, 3 sc in next dc; rep from * 3 times more, ending with sl st in first sc at beg of rnd.

Rnd 2: Sl st in next sc, ch 1, 3 sc in same sc; * sk next sc, sc in next sc, sc in sc just skipped, sk st already worked in; rep from * across row to center sc of corner grp; 3 sc in center sc; rep from first * across row and work rem 3 sides to correspond; end with sl st in first sc at beg of rnd.

Rep Rnd 2 until border measures 2½ inches; fasten off.

DAMSON BORDER: *Rnd 1:* With right side facing, join damson in center sc on any 3-sc grp, ch 1, sc in same st; ch 3, in same st work 3 dc; * in next st work **sc, ch 3, 3 dc—slanted shell made;** sk next 3 sts; rep from * across to 3-sc corner grp. (In next sc work sc, ch 3, 3 dc) 3 times—corner made; sk next 3 sts; rep from first * across next side to 3 corner sts; work corner. Work rem 2 sides to correspond; ending sc in last sc in rnd, ch 3, 3 dc in same st to complete first corner; join with sl st to first sc at beg of rnd; ch 3, turn.

Rnd 2: * Sk next 3 dc, in next ch-3 lp work sc, ch 3, 3 dc; rep from * around; join with sl st to first sc at beg of rnd (following the ch-3 lp); ch 1, turn.

Place markers on ch-3 lps of 3 corners to establish corners.

Rnd 3: In same st as join, work sc, ch 3, 3 dc—(place marker on sc) corner made; * in next ch-3 lp work sc, ch 3, 3 dc; rep from * to marked corner lp; in corner lp work sc, ch 3, 3 dc (place marker on sc); in sc following the marked shell, make sc, ch 3, 3 dc; rep from first * to next marked corner lp; work sc, ch 3, 3 dc in marked lp (place marker on sc); work rem 2 sides to correspond, ending join with sl st to first sc; ch 3, turn.

Rnd 4: Rep Rnd 2; ch 3, turn.

Rnd 5: Work slanted shell in next ch-3 lp, work slanted shell in next sc (mark sc for corner); * work slanted shell in each ch-3 lp to marked sc; slanted shell in next sc (mark sc for corner); rep

from * around; join with sl st to first sc; ch 3, turn.

Rnds 6–9: Rep rnds 2 and 3 alternately; at end of Rnd 9 sl st in top of ch-3, ch 1, turn.

Rnd 10: * Sc in next 3 dc and into ch-3 lp, ch 2; rep from * around, ending sl st in first sc; fasten off.

GREEN BORDER: *Rnd 1:* With right side facing, join green in any sc, ch 3, dc in each dc around (sk ch-2 lps). In corners work 2 dc in ch-2 lps as necessary. (*Note:* Corners are not square; work dcs in lps only to make work lie flat.) Join with sl st to top of ch-3 at beg of rnd.

Rnd 2: Ch 1, sc in same st as join, work sc in each dc around; join to first sc; fasten off. Block again.

Crocheted Chimney Sweep Afghan

Shown on pages 26 and 27.

Finished size is 54x73 inches.

MATERIALS
Coats & Clark Wintuk 4-ply knitting yarn (3½-ounce skeins): 7 skeins of No. 111 eggshell and 3 skeins *each* of No. 602 dark gold, No. 282 rust, No. 818 blue jewel, and No. 814 robin blue
Size H aluminum crochet hook
Blunt-end tapestry needle

Abbreviations: See page 73.
Gauge: One square measures 6¼x6¼ inches.

INSTRUCTIONS
SQUARE MOTIF (make 85): Beg at center, ch 5, join with sl st to form ring.

Rnd 1: Ch 1, work 12 sc in ring; join with sl st to first sc.

Rnd 2: (Ch 4, to count as trc; trc in each of next 2 sc, ch 4, sl st in next sc) 4 times, join last ch-4 to same st as join at beg of rnd; fasten off.

continued

PATCHWORK PATTERNS

Rnd 3: Join new color in last ch-4 lp made; (ch 4, 2 trc in same lp, sl st in top of next ch-4, ch 4, trc in next 2 trc, ch 4, sl st in next ch-4 lp) 4 times, join last ch-4 in top of first ch-4; fasten off.

Rnd 4: Join new color in last ch-4 lp made. * Ch 4, 2 trc in same lp, (sl st in top of next ch-4, ch 4, trc in each of next 2 trc) twice; ch 4, sl st in next ch-4 lp, rep from * 3 times more, join last ch-4 in top of first ch-4; fasten off.

Rnd 5: Join new color in last ch-4 lp made. * Ch 4, 2 trc in same lp, (sl st in top of next ch-4, ch 4, trc in each of next 2 trc) 3 times; ch 4, sl st in next ch-4 lp, rep from * 3 times more, join last ch-4 in top of first ch-4; fasten off.

Rnd 6: Join ecru in last ch-4 lp made, ch 1, in same lp work sc, hdc, dc, trc; * (sc in top of next ch-4, hdc in next trc, in next trc work dc *and* trc) 3 times, sc in top of next ch-4, hdc in same st, in next trc work dc, ch 2, dc; in next trc work hdc and sc; in next ch-4 lp work sc, hdc, dc, trc; rep from * 3 times more; join with sl st to first sc; fasten off.

TRIANGLE MOTIF (make 24):
Row 1: Beg at long edge, ch 16; sl st in eighth ch from hook, ch 4, trc in next 2 ch, ch 4, sl st in next ch, ch 4, sl st in last ch; fasten off; do not turn.

Row 2: Join new color in ch-lp at beg of Row 1, ch 8, sl st in same lp used for join; ch 4, 2 trc in same lp, sl st in top of next ch-4, ch 4, trc in next 2 trc; ch 4, sl st in next ch-4 lp, ch 4, 2 trc in same lp; sl st in fourth ch of ch-8 lp, ch 8, sl st in same ch; fasten off; do not turn.

Row 3: Join new color in fourth ch of ch-8 lp at beg of Row 2, ch 8, sl st in same lp, ch 4, 2 trc in same lp, (sl st in top of ch-4, ch 4, trc in each of next 2 trc) twice; ch 4, sl st in next ch-4 lp, ch 4, 2 trc in same lp, sl st in top of next ch-4, ch 4, trc in next 2 trc, sl st in fourth ch of ch-8 lp, ch 8, sl st in same ch of ch-8 lp; fasten off; do not turn.

Row 4: Join new color in fourth ch of ch-8 lp at beg of Row 3, ch 8, sl st in same lp, ch 4, 2 trc in same lp, (sl st in top of ch-4, ch 4, trc in each of next 2 trc) 3 times, ch 4, sl st in next ch-4 lp, ch 4, 2 trc in same lp, (sl st in top of ch-4, ch 4, trc in each of next 2 trc) twice; sl st in fourth ch of ch-8 lp, ch 8, sl st in next ch of ch-8 lp; fasten off; do not turn.

Row 5: Join ecru in fourth ch of ch-8 lp at beg of last row, ch 3, dc in same ch used for join; in rem ch-lp work sc, hdc, dc, trc; (sc in top of next ch-4, hdc in next trc, in next trc work dc *and* trc) 3 times; sc in top of next ch-4, hdc in same st, in next trc work dc, ch 2, dc, in next trc work hdc *and* sc, in next ch-4 lp work sc, hdc, dc, trc, rep bet ( )s 3 times; sc in fourth ch of ch-8 lp, ch 2, dc in same ch used for last sc. *Working along long edge of triangle,* ch 2, sc in same st as last dc, (ch 3, sc in next join) 4 times, ch 3, sk 2 trc, sc in base of next trc, (ch 3, sc in end of next ch-lp) 4 times, ch 2, sl st into second ch at beg of row; fasten off.

ASSEMBLY: With ecru and working under *both* loops, whip-stitch blocks together using diagram, *left,* as a guide.

BORDER: With right side facing, join ecru in any st of any corner block. Ch 3, and work dc in each st of every corner block. In the triangle edges around, work 2 dc in each ch-3 lp, dc in next sc. Adjust to keep work lying flat; join to top of ch-3 at beg of rnd.

Next rnd: Ch 3, dc in each dc around, join to first dc.

Final rnd: Working *clockwise,* sc in same st as join, * ch 1, sk next dc, sc in next dc; rep from * around; join to first sc; fasten off.

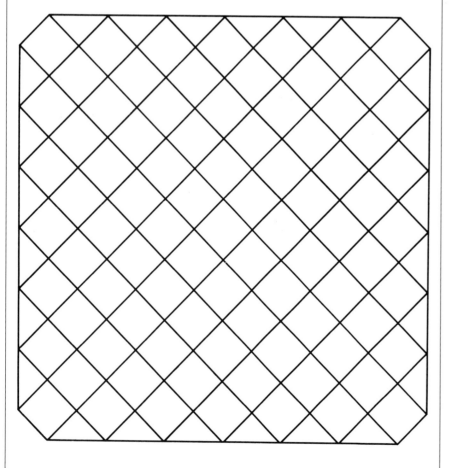

Cross-Stitched Rose Afghan

Shown on page 28.

Finished size, including border, is 58x70 inches.

MATERIALS:

Bucilla Softex worsted-weight yarn (4-ounce balls): 15 balls of No. 5 winter white
Sport-weight yarn (1¾-ounce balls) for cross-stitch embroidery: 3 balls of tea rose; 2 balls *each* of dusty rose and light terra-cotta; 1 ball *each* of light sage, sage, dark pine, pale lavender, dark lavender, and sky blue; and scraps of dark yellow
Size G afghan crochet hook
Size H aluminum crochet hook
8 yards *each* of 5 colors of ⅜-inch-wide satin ribbon (to match cross-stitch designs)
Blunt-end tapestry needle

Abbreviations: See page 73.
Gauge: 5 afghan stitches = 1 inch.

INSTRUCTIONS
Crocheting the afghan

PANEL (make 4): With winter white yarn and afghan hook, ch 61.

First Half of Row 1: Leaving all lps on hook, sk first ch, * insert hook in next ch, yo, draw up lp; rep from * in each ch across—61 lps on hook.

Second Half of Row 1: Yo and draw through first lp on hook, * yo, draw through next 2 lps on hook; rep from * until 1 lp rem on hook.

First Half of Row 2: Insert hook under *second* vertical bar of Row 1, yo, draw up lp and leave on hook; * insert hook in next vertical bar, yo, draw up lp and leave on hook; rep from * across row to within 1 bar of end; insert hook under last bar and thread behind it, yo, draw up lp—61 lps on hook.

Second Half of Row 2: Rep Second Half of Row 1. Rep Row 2 (first and second halves) until 182 rows are completed.

Last row: Draw up lp under second vertical bar and draw through lp on hook; * draw up lp in next vertical bar and draw through lp on hook; rep from * across to within 1 bar of end; insert hook under last bar and thread behind it, draw up lp and draw through lp on hook; fasten off. Carefully block all panels.

ASSEMBLY: Align rows; whipstitch panels with off-white yarn.

Cross-stitching the rose design

Referring to chart, *below*, work the rose motif over each panel, using the tapestry needle and 1 strand of sport yarn. Begin on second row at lower edge of left panel and work rose motif 6 times to top of left panel (1 row should remain unworked).

continued

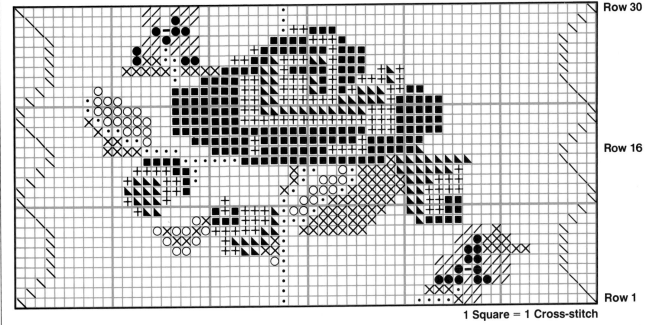

Row 30

Row 16

Row 1

1 Square = 1 Cross-stitch

COLOR KEY

⊡ Dark pine
⊠ Sage
◯ Light sage
◣ Light terracotta

⊞ Tea rose
■ Dusty rose
◩ Pale lavender

◕ Dark lavender
⊟ Dark yellow
◸ Sky blue

Work motifs on second panel, *except* begin to work from chart at Row 16 on the second row of panel. Complete the upper half of the motif, then work remainder of second panel with complete motifs (see photograph, page 28). Finish last motif with first 15 rows of chart (1 row should remain unworked).

Work the third panel in same manner as first panel, and fourth panel in same manner as second panel.

Crocheting the border

Rnd 1: With Size H crochet hook, right side facing, sc in each st around, working 3 sc in each corner st. (To keep work flat, you may have to work 1 sc in every other st on short sides.) Join with sl st to first sc, ch 1.

Rnd 2: Work 2 sc in each sc around, working 3 sc in each corner st; join with sl st to first sc.

Rnd 3: Work sc in each sc around, working 3 sc in corner st.

Rnd 4: Ch 5, sk 2 sc, dc in next sc; * ch 2, sk 2 sc, dc in next sc; rep from * around; end ch 2, sl st to third ch of ch-5 at beg of rnd.

Rnd 5: Ch 5, * dc in next dc, ch 2; rep from * to corner sp; dc in corner sp, ch 2; rep from first * around; end with sl st in third ch of ch-5 at beg of rnd.

Rnds 6–8: Rep Rnd 5.

Rnd 9: Ch 4, dc in first sp, **ch 3, sl st in third ch from hook—picot made;** dc in same sp, ch 1, dc in same sp, ch 1; * sl st in next sp, ch 1, in next sp work (dc, ch 1, dc, picot, dc, ch 1, dc, ch 1); rep from * around; end with sl st in last sp, ch 1, sl st in third ch of beg ch-4; fasten off.

Using 1 color of ribbon for each of the 5-dc rnds, cut 4 lengths to fit along each side, allowing an additional 18 inches for bows in each corner end. Weave ribbons over and under the dcs along the sides; tie ribbons into bows.

Crocheted Afghan With Cross-Stitched Houses and Stars

Shown on page 29.

Finished size is 45x45 inches.

MATERIALS
Unger Roly Poly (3½-ounce balls): 6 balls of No. 9578 off-white, 3 balls of No. 126 grape heather, and 1 ball of No. 124 blue-green heather
Size H afghan crochet hook, or size to obtain gauge
Size G aluminum crochet hook
Blunt-end tapestry needle

Abbreviations: See page 74.
Gauge: With Size H hook, 4 sts = 1 inch; 4 rows afghan st = 1 inch.

INSTRUCTIONS

BLOCK (make 9): With off-white and afghan hook, ch 41.

First Half of Row 1: Leaving all lps on hook, sk first ch, * insert hook in next ch, yo, draw up lp; rep from * in each ch across—41 lps on hook.

Second Half of Row 1: Yo and draw through first lp on hook, * yo, draw through 2 lps on hook; rep from * until 1 lp rem on hook.

First Half of Row 2: Insert hook under *second* vertical bar of Row 1, yo, draw up lp and leave on hook; * insert hook in next vertical bar, yo, draw up lp and leave on hook; rep from * across row to 1 bar of end; insert hook under last bar and thread behind it, yo, draw up lp—41 lps on hook.

Second Half of Row 2: Rep Second Half of Row 1. Rep Row 2 (first and second halves) for 40 rows:

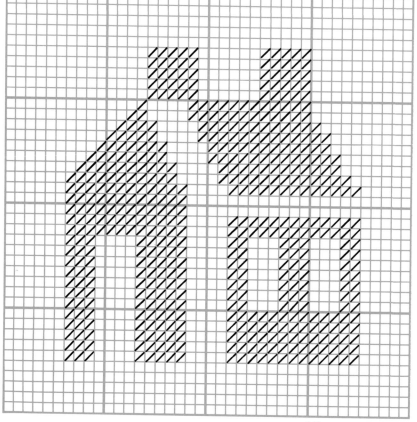

1 Square = 1 Stitch

Last row: Draw up lp under second vertical bar and draw through lp on hook—1 lp rem on hook; * draw up lp in next vertical bar and draw through lp on hook—1 lp rem on hook; rep from * across to within 1 bar of end; insert hook under last bar and thread behind it, draw up lp and draw through last lp on hook; fasten off.

Cross-stitching the star and house blocks

Thread needle with single strand of yarn. Work cross-stitches over the vertical bars. (*Note:* The *top* stitch of each cross-stitch should be worked in the *same* direction throughout.)

Refer to chart, page 40, and work house motif on 5 blocks, using blue-green heather yarn. Using chart, *below,* work star motif on 4 blocks using grape heather yarn. Locate the center of the designs on the charts and the center of the crocheted pieces; begin stitching here.

BORDERS AROUND BLOCKS: Work edging on left and right *sides* only of each block.

Row 1: With right side facing and Size G hook, join grape in lower right corner, ch 3; working in end of each row, dc evenly across side edge of block to next corner *and at same time,* work decs as necessary to keep work flat. (To dec: Work dc to point where 2 lps rem on hook, yo, draw up lp in *next* dc, yo, draw through 2 lps on hook, yo, draw through 3 lps on hook.) At end of row, ch 3, turn.

Row 2: Dc in next dc and each dc across. Ch 1, turn.

Row 3: Sc in each dc; fasten off.

Rep rows 1–3 on left side of same block.

Work side edgings on all rem motifs.

Using photograph, page 29, as a guide, sew 3 blocks tog for top strip (house, star, house); assemble middle and bottom strips. Work 3 rows of border edging as for side edging along entire top

and bottom of joined strips. Sew 3 strips tog.

Next rnd: Join grape in st at lower left corner; ch 3, 4 dc in same st as join, * work 126 dc across edge to next corner, *and at same time* dec where necessary to keep work flat, work 5 dc in corner, work 142 dc across next edge to corner; rep from * around; join to top of ch-3.

Work 2 more rnds of dc, working 5 dc in each corner st. At end of last rnd, fasten off.

OUTSIDE BORDER: With off-white, work 1 more rnd of dc, working 5 dc in each corner st.

Next rnd: Ch 3, dc in next st, * **dc around post from front of next 2 dc—raised dc made,** dc in next 2 sts; rep from * around, working 5 dc in each corner st; join to top of ch-3.

Next 3 rnds: Ch 3, working in pat as established, work raised dc over raised dcs, dc over dcs, and 5 dc in each corner st; join to top of ch-3. (*Note*: Add raised dcs in corner sts as work increases.)

SCALLOPED EDGING: *Rnd 1:* Ch 3, * sk 2 sts, sc in next st, sk 2 sts, dc in next st, in next st work (dc, 3 trc, and dc), dc in next st; rep from * around, working (dc, 5 trc, and dc) in each corner st; end dc, 3 trc, and dc in last st; join to top of beg ch-3.

Rnd 2: * Sk next sc, sc in next 3 sts, in center trc work (hdc, ch 2, hdc), sc in next 3 sts; rep from * around, working sc in 4 sts to center trc at corner; in corner trc work (2 hdc, ch 2, and 2 hdc); join to first sc; fasten off.

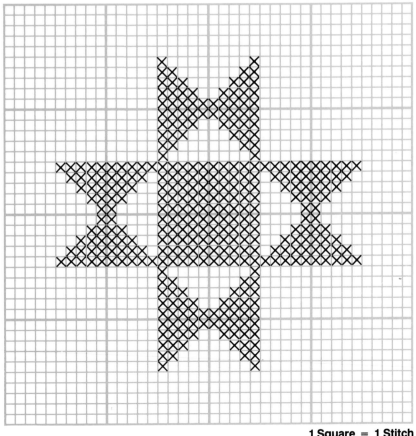

1 Square = 1 Stitch

Knitted Victorian Crazy Quilt Afghan

Shown on pages 30 and 31.

Finished afghan is 39 inches square, excluding fringe.

MATERIALS

Brunswick Pomfret sport yarn (50-gram balls): 5 balls of No. 558 blueberry heather (A); 2 balls of No. 5031 medium yellow (B); and 1 ball *each* of No. 5741 rust heather (C), No. 557 cranberry (D), No. 564 pewter heather (E), No. 544 dartmouth green (F), and No. 597 amethyst heather (G)

Scraps of 3-ply persian yarn in assorted colors

Size 5 knitting needles

Blunt-end tapestry needle

Size F aluminum crochet hook

Abbreviations: See pages 73 and 77.

Gauge: Working in stockinette st, 6 sts = 1 inch; 7 rows = 1 inch.

INSTRUCTIONS

KNITTED PANEL (make 6): Following chart, *right,* for color placement, cast on 38 sts. Work even in stockinette st (k 1 row, p 1 row) for 6 inches (approximately 42 rows); change to next color and work for 6 more inches. Continue in this manner, changing colors as you work until strip has 6 color blocks; bind off.

Work rem 5 panels as above.

EMBROIDERY: Using 2 plies of persian yarn, locate center of design and center of pattern and begin to embroider here. Work designs in duplicate st (see page 17) on every other block, following diagrams, page 43. Use colors of your choice, or colors in color key.

For interest, flop designs of dog and bow. Add white French knot for eye on black dog and black French knot for white dog.

Shadings on the apple and pear are accomplished by working 1 strand of fruit color with 1 strand of shading color.

ASSEMBLY: With right sides facing, sew embroidered strips together, being careful to align blocks.

EMBROIDERY: Embroider over seams and color changes between blocks, using single strand of persian yarn. See pages 44 and 45 for stitch diagrams. Combine colors and stitches to obtain interesting results. See photograph, pages 30 and 31, for ideas.

BORDER: *Rnd 1:* With right side facing and Size F crochet hook, join blueberry yarn in top left corner and work sc evenly spaced around, working 3 sc in each corner st; join with sl st to first sc; ch 1, turn.

Rnd 2: Sc in each sc around, working 3 sc in corner sts; join; ch 1, turn. Rep Rnd 2 until border measures 1 inch from beg.

Next rnd: Work 1 more rnd of sc, *except* along top and bottom edges of afghan work sc, * ch 2, sk 2 sc, sc in next 4 sc, rep from * to end of side, adjusting work to make the ch-2 and the sc in corner st come out even. Work rem sides to correspond; join.

FRINGE: In bundles of 7, knot 9-inch strands of blueberry yarn along top and bottom edges in ch-2 sp of last rnd.

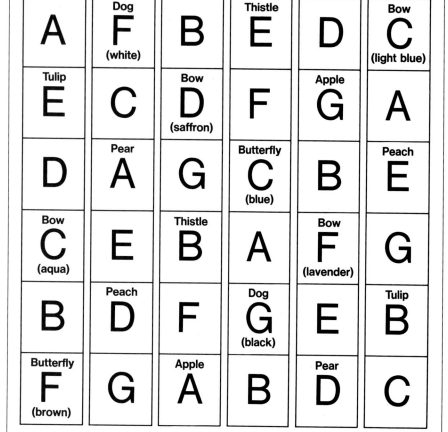

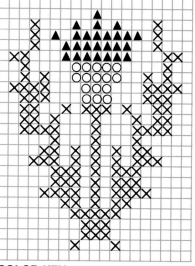

COLOR KEY
▲ Rose
◯ Brown
⊠ Dark olive green

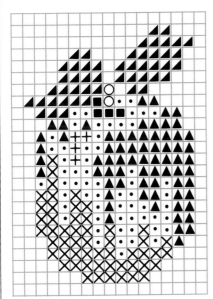

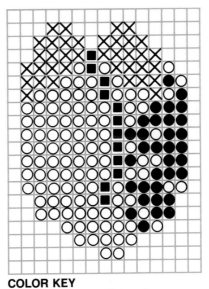

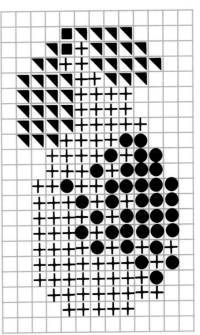

COLOR KEY
- ⊡ Red
- ⊠ Shaded red
- ▲ Burgundy
- ⊞ White
- ■ Brown
- ○ Black
- ◨ Olive green

COLOR KEY
- ⊠ Green
- ■ Light brown
- ○ Peach
- ● Shaded peach

COLOR KEY
- ⊞ Gold
- ● Shaded gold
- ■ Black
- ◨ Olive green

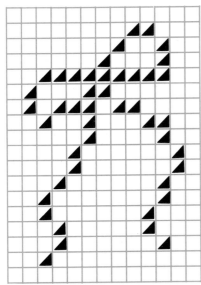

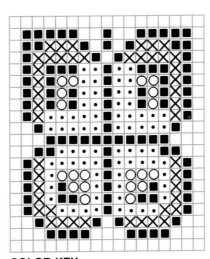

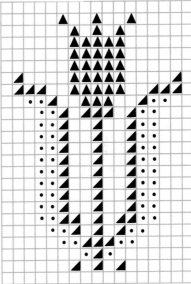

COLOR KEY
- ◨ Light blue .... Lavender
  Saffron .... Aqua

COLOR KEY
- ■ Navy .... Black
- ⊠ Dark grey .... Brown
- ⊡ Light grey .... Peach
- ○ White .... White

COLOR KEY
- ◨ Green
- ⊡ Forest green
- ▲ Burgundy

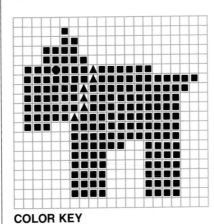

COLOR KEY
- ■ Black .... White
- ● White .... Black
- ▲ Blue .... Turquoise

PATCHWORK PATTERNS

Embroidery Stitches

Backstitch

Buttonhole stitch

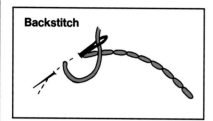

Chain stitch and variations

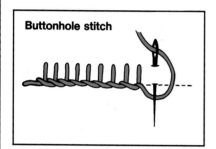

Chain scroll

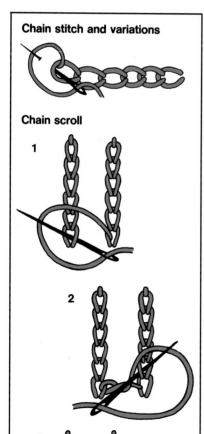

1

2

3

Cable chain stitch

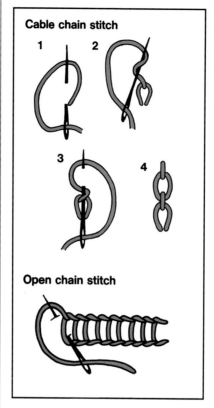

1   2

3   4

Open chain stitch

Couching stitch

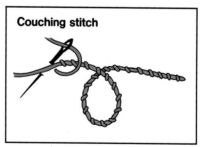

Cross-stitch

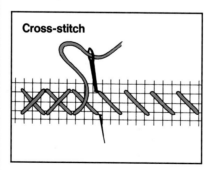

Darning stitch

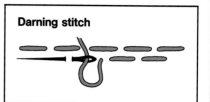

Featherstitch and variations

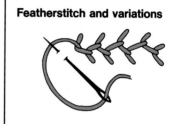

Long-armed featherstitch

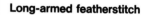

Parallel featherstitch

Single featherstitch

Fly stitch

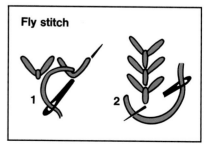

1   2

French knot

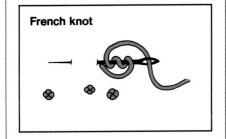

Harringbone stitch

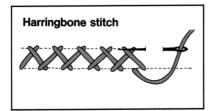

Laid work

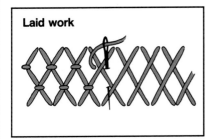

Lazy daisy stitch

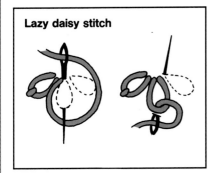

Outline stitch

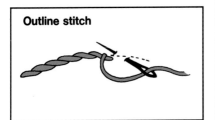

Tips for Working with Yarns

Here are some tips and techniques to help you make yarn substitutions, sew seams, finish yarn ends, and block your projects successfully.

SUBSTITUTING YARN: Any yarn can be substituted for any other yarn, provided you can work it to the gauge specified in the pattern. If you want your project to look like the project pictured, however, select a yarn of similar weight and texture to the yarn noted in the Materials list.

When substituting, you need to determine how much of the new yarn you will need. First, multiply the number of yards per skein in the *pattern* yarn by the number of skeins required. Then, divide this number by the number of yards per skein of the *substitute* yarn to determine the number of skeins needed in the new yarn.

SEAMING: Sew seams with the yarn used in the project, except when the project yarn is nubby, thick and thin, or bulky. For projects made with these yarns, select a smooth, uniformly twisted, medium-weight yarn in a matching color. If the color is difficult to match, use crewel yarns; they are available in a range of colors and can be separated into strands.

The tension of all seam finishes must be tight enough to hide the joining stitches, but loose enough to be as elastic as the finished item.

To join, pin two sections together, matching design lines or pattern stitches. Then stitch, using backstitches, overcast stitches, or whipstitches.

Backstitches are firm and strong, but they must be worked at the correct tension because they have little "give" once in place. Whipstitches or overcast stitches result in a flat, almost invisible seam; they are especially useful for joining motifs such as Granny Squares. Because they are flat, whipstitches work best on knitted panels with seed- or garter-stitch edges.

FINISHING ENDS: When breaking off yarn ends, leave at least a 6-inch tail for weaving. When working in rows, weave yarn ends into the seam allowances whenever possible. When working in rounds, weave ends *vertically* to make them less noticeable on the right side.

Split the ends of bulky yarns into plies; weave each ply separately for a finer appearance on the right side.

BLOCKING: Before blocking, check the label of the yarn you are using; you may find that the yarn requires no blocking. If blocking is needed, follow the manufacturer's instructions.

Projects may be blocked before or after seaming. To block before seaming, pin matching pieces to identical shape and size. Place a wet or dry press cloth over each piece and, supporting the weight of the iron at all times, allow steam from the iron to penetrate the fabric. Or, pin each section to shape, mist lightly with water, and allow to dry.

To block a project after joining, pin the item to the finished measurements, then block it following the procedures explained above.

CLASSIC FAVORITES

IN BOTH TECHNIQUES

Ask any group of crocheters and knitters what projects they like to make most, and chances are they'll answer "Afghans." Some patterns are perennial favorites, admired by stitchers of every degree of skill and experience. Ripple designs, plaids, checks, argyles, and beautifully textured fisherman styles head the list of these time-honored treasures. In this section, you'll find examples of each to stitch in your favorite technique.

The wavy pattern characteristic of ripple-style afghans is an easy one to knit or crochet. In both techniques, only two rows of stitches establish the pattern. Then, simply by changing yarn colors, you create the overall design.

The bands or "waves" of color may be uniformly sized and repeated in the same sequence down the length of the throw. Or, you may vary the width of the waves and eliminate any repetition, as in the afghan shown here. Either way, ripple designs bring warmth and vitality to virtually every decorating scheme.

Soft grays, green, and shades of rust enliven this 50x72-inch knitted ripple design. The waves of color range from two to 16 rows deep, and the colors follow one another randomly rather than in a regular repeat.

How-to instructions begin on page 60.

CLASSIC FAVORITES

Traditionally, the waves in ripple designs run parallel to the shorter sides of an afghan. But by exercising some creative license, you can turn the waves on end, and craft an unconventional version of this classic pattern.

Worked in the vibrant colors often found in Matisse paintings, this 53x64-inch throw features a pair of double crochet clusters at the peaks of the zigzag stripes. Tassels in the same bright yarns used for the stripes edge the ends of the afghan.

To adapt this design to the more conventional horizontal stripes, begin with a shorter foundation chain, and work for a suitable length.

Traditionally, the afghan stitch is used to crochet plain panels, which then are embellished with embroidery. But the houndstooth design, *opposite*, is an imaginative departure from this technique. By working with *two* yarn colors, you can stitch the checks into the fabric as you make this 43½x60-inch throw.

Dynamic colors and oversize checks give the knitted design, *above*, lots of impact. And, like the crocheted houndstooth pattern, this 36x60-inch afghan is worked using two colors at once. Here, the color not in use is carried across the *back* of the work, rather than *beneath* the stitches.

Beginning knitters will find this afghan easy to make, because it is worked in stockinette stitch (knit one row, purl one row) accented with a simple-to-master garter-stitch border.

CLASSIC FAVORITES

A plaid similar to a gingham check, but featuring black instead of white as the contrasting color, is called buffalo plaid.

Knitting a buffalo plaid, shown on the afghan, *opposite,* is easy when you work with two strands of yarn at once. The solid black and teal checks in the pattern are worked with two strands of the same color. A strand of each color worked together forms the remaining checks in this 48x60-inch design.

Color changes on this crocheted plaid afghan, *above,* only *look* complicated. Actually, the design is worked in seven vertical panels, and color changes are worked as horizontal stripes. (Some of the colors in this 48x59-inch throw are worked in pattern stitches to add interest to the design.)

A green edging along each panel and rows of chain stitches in contrasting colors provide the perpendicular stripes.

CLASSIC FAVORITES

Two traditional Scottish designs—glen plaid and rows of blooming thistles—are knitted into the afghan shown here.

This 47x59-inch afghan is knitted in rounds. Because you always have the right side of the work facing you while working in rounds, all color changes are made on the back of the work. A purled ridge marks the left and right side edges.

After the afghan is complete (it will actually be tube-shaped), rows of machine-zigzag stitches secure the stitches and mark the line for slashing. Sew a knitted facing, worked on smaller needles, along the sides to conceal the raw edges.

Heather-colored yarn is an appropriate choice for the tassel-style fringe.

CLASSIC FAVORITES

Not just for hand-knit socks and vests, the classic argyle pattern is an ideal one for afghans, as well.

The knitted version, *left*, varies slightly from the usual argyle pattern because it is worked in only two colors. Argyle diamonds, here styled to be almost square, alternate with diamonds knitted in a flecked pattern. The result is a lively design that's tailor-made for two-color knitting that measures 48x66 inches.

In contrast, the crocheted argyle, *above*, is worked with oversize, elongated diamonds in purple and camel. Use a surface slip-stitch technique (explained in the instructions) for the

burgundy crisscrossing lines. This design measures 50x60 inches.

Like houndstooth check afghans, these designs can be stitched in a splendid assortment of color schemes, making them suitable for any decor.

CLASSIC FAVORITES

I rish seafaring clans are credited with creating the beautifully intricate fisherman-knit styles. The patterns are so distinctive that individual families laid claim to their own combination of cables, twists, and other stitches.

Worked in a seashore blue, the knitted fisherman afghan, *far left,* is an excellent sampling of traditional pattern stitches. In addition to seed-stitch accents, this 52x64-inch design features plaited cables, horseshoe cables, honeycomb work, trinity stitch (which forms a pebbly texture), and a connecting diamond pattern.

Crocheters can enjoy working the lush textures of fisherman knitting, too. The 57x59-inch afghan, *left,* is composed of crochet stitches designed to imitate the intricacies of the knitted patterns. The broad center panel is worked with raised treble crochet stitches to form interlocking diamonds. Other panels feature popcorns arranged in diamonds, and raised stitches to form cables. The dividing panels and border are worked in a bead stitch in subtly contrasting colors.

Knitted Ripple Afghan

Shown on pages 46 and 47.

Finished size is 50x72 inches.

MATERIALS
Unger Aries knitting worsted yarn (3½-ounce balls): 4 balls of No. 430 rust, No. 470 terra cotta, No. 458 oatmeal, No. 549 pink, No. 469 light gray, No. 472 peach, and No. 524 olive green
Size 9 circular 22-inch knitting needle
Size G aluminum crochet hook

Abbreviations: See pages 73 and 77.
Gauge: 9 sts = 2 inches; 9 rows = 2 inches.

INSTRUCTIONS
Work afghan in color bands of your choice (always working an even number of rows in each color band), or to make the afghan shown on page 52, work in the following color sequence: 4 rows rust, 4 rows terra cotta, 8 rows oatmeal, 2 rows pink, 16 rows light gray, 2 rows peach, 4 rows terra cotta, 8 rows olive green, 2 rows pink, 14 rows peach, 2 rows rust, 4 rows light gray, 2 rows terra cotta, 8 rows oatmeal, 2 rows light gray, 16 rows olive green, 2 rows rust, 4 rows peach, 2 rows pink, 4 rows light gray, 8 rows peach, 2 rows terra cotta, 14 rows oatmeal, 2 rows terra cotta, 4 rows olive green, 8 rows oatmeal, 2 rows olive green, 16 rows pink, 2 rows rust, 8 rows light gray, 4 rows peach, 2 rows terra cotta, 16 rows oatmeal, 2 rows terra cotta, 8 rows peach, 4 rows light gray, 2 rows pink, 4 rows peach, 2 rows rust, 16 rows olive green, 2 rows light gray, 6 rows oatmeal, 4 rows pink, 2 rows terra cotta, 4 rows light gray, 2 rows rust, 16 rows peach, 2 rows pink, 8 rows olive green, 4 rows terra cotta, 2 rows oatmeal, 4 rows olive green, 2 rows pink, 16 rows light gray, 2 rows peach, 8 rows oatmeal, 4 rows terra cotta, 4 rows rust.
With rust, cast on 227 sts.

Row 1 (right side): K 3, sl 1, k 1, psso, * k 19, sl 2 as if to k, k 1, p2sso. Rep from * 8 times more—24 sts rem; end k 19, k 2 tog, k 3.
Row 2: K 3, p 10; **insert tip of right-hand needle under running thread before next st, leaving lp on right-hand needle—make 1 (M1) made;** p 1, M1, p 19. Rep from * 8 times more—14 sts rem; end M1, p 1, M1, p 10, k 3.
Working in color sequence as cited above, rep rows 1 and 2 for pat. Bind off rust.

EDGING: With crochet hook and right side facing, attach rust yarn at right-hand edge of 1 short end of afghan. Ch 2, hdc in each of first 3 sts; working hdc across, make (hdc, ch 2, hdc) at "peaks" and sk 2 sts at "valleys," ending with hdc in last 3 sts; ch 2, turn.
Next row: Work hdc as above, working (hdc, ch 4, sl st in fourth ch from hook for picot, hdc) in each ch-2 sp in the "peaks" and sk 2 hdc at "valleys." Fasten off. Rep edging on opposite end.

FRINGE: From the oatmeal, cut 420 sixteen-inch lengths of yarn and in bundles of 10 strands, knot fringe on both short edges, placing a bundle in each peak and valley.

Crocheted Ripple Afghan

Shown on pages 48 and 49.

Finished size is 53x64 inches, excluding fringe.

MATERIALS
Berger du Nord "Sport" worsted yarn (100-gram balls): 10 balls of No. 6381 ecru and 2 balls *each* of No. 7632 mustard, No. 7624 purple, No. 7291 fuchsia, No. 8236 red, No. 8232 coral, No. 7869 blue, No. 7416 pewter, and No. 8226 green
Size I aluminum crochet hook

Abbreviations: See page 73.
Gauge: 3 dc = 1 inch; 2 dc rows = 1½ inches.

INSTRUCTIONS
With ecru, ch 172.
Row 1: Dc in fourth ch from hook and next 3 ch, 2 dc in next ch; * ch 2, sk next 2 ch, in next ch work **3 dc, ch 2, 3 dc—shell made;** ch 2, sk next 2 ch, 2 dc in next ch, dc in next 4 ch, sk 2 ch, dc in next 4 ch, 2 dc in next ch; rep from * 8 times more; end ch 2, sk 2 ch, shell in next ch, ch 2, sk 2 ch, 2 dc in next ch, dc in next 5 ch; ch 3, turn.
Row 2: Sk first dc, dc in next 5 dc, 2 dc in next dc; * ch 2, sk next ch-2 lp, shell in ch-2 sp of next shell, ch 2, sk next ch-2 lp, 2 dc in next dc, dc in next 4 dc, sk 2 dc, dc in next 4 dc, 2 dc in next dc; rep from * 8 times more; end ch 2, sk next ch-2 lp; shell in ch-2 sp of next shell, ch 2, sk next ch-2 lp, 2 dc in next dc, dc in next 5 dc; fasten off ecru, turn.
Row 3: With color of your choice, join yarn in top of first dc, ch 3, dc in next 5 dc, 2 dc in next dc; * ch 2, sk next ch-2 lp, shell in ch-2 sp of next shell, ch 2, sk next ch-2 lp, 2 dc in next dc, dc in next 4 dc, sk 2 dc, dc in next 4 dc, 2 dc in next dc; rep from * 8 times more; end ch 2, sk next ch-2 lp; shell in ch-2 sp of next shell, ch 2, sk next ch-2 lp, 2 dc in next dc, dc in next 5 dc; fasten off yarn, turn.
Row 4: With color of your choice, rep Row 3.
Row 5: With ecru, rep Row 3; do not fasten off at end of row, ch 3, turn.
Row 6: Rep Row 2.
Rep rows 3–6 for pat 18 times more or until desired width. Tie in ends at ends of rows.

FRINGE: Cut 8 strands of colored yarn, each 12 inches long. Double these strands to form a loop. With right side of afghan facing, insert crochet hook from back to front in end st along long side at end of corresponding color row and draw lp through; then draw loose ends through lp and pull up tightly to form a knot. Knot 8 strands in end of every colored row along this edge.
Work fringe along opposite side edge in same way. Trim fringe.

Crocheted Houndstooth Afghan

Shown on page 50.

Finished size is 43½x60 inches.

MATERIALS
Coats & Clark Royal Mouliné knitting worsted (50-gram balls): 15 balls of No. 6018 slate, 13 balls of No. 6020 white, and 6 balls of No. 6001 red
Size 10½ afghan hook with extender
Size J aluminum crochet hook

Abbreviations: See page 73.
Gauge: 5 afghan sts = 1 inch; 7 rows = 1 inch.

INSTRUCTIONS
Note: Each complete row of afghan stitches consists of 2 parts—the first half of the row and the second half of the row.

STRIPE SECTION: *Foundation row:* With afghan hook and slate, ch 217. Mark starting chain for lower edge of afghan.
First Half of Row 1: Retaining all lps on hook, sk first ch, * insert hook in next ch, yo, draw up lp; rep from * across row—217 lps on hook.
Second Half of Row 1: Yo and draw through first lp on hook, * yo, draw through 2 lps on hook; rep from * until 1 lp rem on hook.
First Half of Row 2: Insert hook under *second* vertical bar of Row 1, yo, draw up lp and leave on hook; * insert hook in next vertical bar, yo, draw up lp and leave on hook; rep from * across row to within 1 bar of end; insert hook under last bar and thread behind it, yo, draw up lp—217 lps.
Second Half of Row 2: Rep Second Half of Row 1 until 2 lps rem on hook, drop slate; with white, yo, draw through last 2 lps on hook—color change made at end of Second Half of Row.

Note: Afghan begins to work with 2 yarn colors. Carry and work colors as follows: On first half of every row when making a color change, drop color not in use to back of work and pick up new color; carry the dropped strand along back of work, twisting it around color in use following every 2 drawn up vertical bars. On second half of every row carry unused strand loosely along back of work, twisting around color in use following every 2 lps worked.

FIRST HOUNDSTOOTH SECTION: *First Half of Row 1:* Retaining all lps on hook, with white, draw up lp in second vertical bar and in each of next 2 vertical bars; * drop white, pick up slate, and draw up a lp in next vertical bar; drop slate, pick up white and draw up lp in each of next 3 vertical bars; rep from * to last vertical bar; with white, draw up lp in last bar and through st directly behind it as before.
Second Half of Row 1: With white, yo, draw through 1 lp, (yo, draw through 2 lps) 3 times; * drop white, with slate, yo, draw through 2 lps, drop slate; (with white, yo, draw through 2 lps) 3 times; rep from * across, end last rep (with white, yo, draw through 2 lps) 4 times.
First Half of Row 2: Retaining all lps on hook, with white, draw up lp in second vertical bar and next bar; * drop white, with slate, draw up lp in next bar, drop slate; with white, draw up lp in each of next 3 bars; rep from * across to last 2 bars; with slate, draw up lp in next bar, drop slate; with white, draw up lp in last bar.
Second Half of Row 2: With white, yo, draw through 1 lp; * with slate, yo, draw through 2 lps; (with white, yo, draw through 2 lps) 3 times; rep from * across.

First Half of Row 3: Retaining all lps on hook, with slate, draw up lp in second vertical bar; * with white, draw up lp in next bar; with slate, draw up lp in each of next 3 bars; rep from * to last 3 bars; with white, draw up lp in next bar; with slate, draw up lp in next bar; with white, draw up lp in last bar.
Second Half of Row 3: With white, yo, draw through 1 lp; with slate, yo, draw through 2 lps; * with white, yo, draw through 2 lps; (with slate, yo, draw through 2 lps) 3 times; rep from * to last 3 lps; with white, yo, draw through 2 lps; with slate, yo, draw through 2 lps; with white, yo, draw through last 2 lps.
First Half of Row 4: Retaining all lps on hook, with white, draw up lp in second vertical bar; * with slate, draw up lp in each of next 3 bars; with white, draw up lp in next bar; rep from * to last 3 bars; with slate, draw up lp in each of next 2 bars; with white, draw up lp in last bar.
Second Half of Row 4: With white, yo, draw through 1 lp; (with slate, yo, draw through 2 lps) twice; * with white, yo, draw through 2 lps; (with slate, yo, draw through 2 lps) 3 times; rep from * to last 2 lps; (with white, yo, draw through 2 lps) twice.
First and second halves of rows 5–19: Rep rows 1–4 of Houndstooth pat 3 times more; then rep rows 1–3 of pat once more, changing to red at end of second half of last row; fasten off slate and white.

FIRST RED AND SLATE BORDER: *Rows 1–3:* With red, work in afghan stitch, changing to slate at end of Second Half of Row 3.
First Half of Row 4: Retaining all lps on hook, with slate, draw up lp in second vertical bar and next 108 bars; mark last lp on hook with safety pin for center lp; draw up lp in each rem bar to end of row.

continued

Second Half of Row 4: Yo, draw through 1 lp; * yo, draw through 2 lps; leaving pin on center lp, rep from * across, changing to red at end of row.

Note: As work progresses, continue to transfer pin onto center lp on first half of every row.

Row 5: With red, work even in afghan stitch.

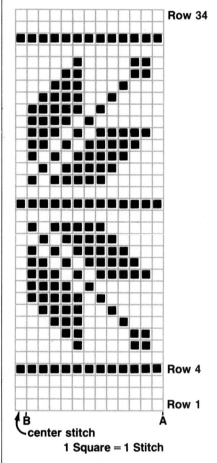

Row 34

Row 4

Row 1

B ⌐center stitch A

1 Square = 1 Stitch

COLOR KEY
■ Slate ☐ Red

Following chart and color key for Border, *above,* work in afghan st, noting the first lp on the hook for the first half of each row is always the first st of the row. When following chart from A to B at the beg of row, the first st is already on the hook; begin working the second st on the chart. Also when following the chart, take care to make appropriate color changes at end of Second Half of rows as necessary.

First Half of Row 6: Carrying and changing colors as already established, work from A to B 9 times; work center lp; then work from B to A 9 times.

Second Half of Row 6: Keeping in same color pat as for First Half of row, work across. Continue to follow chart, working First Half and Second Half of each row in same manner as Row 6 until Row 34 is completed; fasten off red and remove safety pin.

CENTER HOUNDSTOOTH SECTION—*First and second halves of next 4 rows:* Rep First and Second Half of rows 4, 3, 2, and 1 of First Houndstooth Section. Rep last 4 rows until length from starting chain is about 43½ inches, ending with Row 3 of pat; fasten off slate and white.

SECOND RED AND SLATE BORDER: *Rows 1 and 2:* With red, work even in afghan stitch. Following chart for Red and Slate Border work rows 4–34. Do not fasten off red at end of last row.

Last row: With red, work even in afghan stitch; fasten off red and remove safety pin.

LAST HOUNDSTOOTH SECTION: *Rows 1–3:* Rep rows 3, 2, and 1 of First Houndstooth Section. Then rep rows 4, 3, 2, and 1 of First Houndstooth Section 4 times; fasten off white.

Next row: With slate rep Row 2 of Stripe pat.

Last row: Draw up lp in second vertical bar and draw through lp on hook, * draw up lp in next vertical bar and draw through lp on hook; rep from * across row; fasten off.

SIDE EDGING: With right side of 1 long edge of afghan facing and using crochet hook, join white to right-hand corner stitch, ch 1, sc in same place as join. Being careful to keep work flat, with white, sc evenly along end sts of Stripe and Houndstooth pats to within end st before red st of next border pat; * with white, draw up lp in last st, drop white, with red, yo, draw through 2 lps on hook—color change made; fasten off

white. * With red, sc evenly along red border pat to within end st before next Houndstooth pat; change to white in end st; fasten off red. With white, sc evenly along Houndstooth pat to within end st before red border pat; rep from * to corner st; do not change to red at end of last rep. Fasten off.

Work edging along opposite side edge to correspond.

FRINGE: Cut 6 strands of white each 12 inches long. Double these strands to form a loop. With right side of afghan facing, insert crochet hook from back to front in end st on narrow edge and draw lp through; then draw loose ends through lp and pull up tightly to form a knot. Knot 6 strands in every other st along this edge.

Work fringe along opposite narrow edge in same way and trim.

Knitted Houndstooth Afghan

Shown on page 51.

Finished size is 36x60 inches.

MATERIALS
Coats & Clark Red Heart sport yarn (2-ounce skeins): 5 balls of No. 12 black and 4 skeins of No. 905 red
Size 6 knitting needles

Abbreviations: See page 77.
Gauge: 11 sts = 2 inches.

INSTRUCTIONS
With black, cast on 204 sts. Work in garter st (k every row) for 20 rows.

Note: Keeping first and last 10 sts of each row in garter stitch for side borders, work houndstooth pattern in stockinette st (k right-side row, p wrong-side row), carrying colors across row as you work. Read chart from right to left for all odd-number rows and from left to right for all even-number rows.

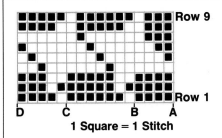

Row 9

Row 1

D   C   B   A

1 Square = 1 Stitch

COLOR KEY
■ Black   □ Red

Row 1 (right side): Knit first 10 sts in garter st with black. Beg to work from chart, *below,* and knit from A to C once; (knit from B to C) 24 times; knit from C to D once; knit last 10 sts for border.

Row 2 (wrong side): Knit first 10 sts for border, purl from D to B once; (purl from C to B) 24 times; purl from B to A once; knit 10 sts for border.

Work through Row 9; then rep rows 1–9 until 43 red motifs are completed, ending with a k row.

Next row: With black, k 10, p 184, k 10.

Next 20 rows: With black, k in garter st; bind off and block.

Knitted Buffalo-Plaid Afghan

Shown on page 52.

Finished size is 48x60 inches.

MATERIALS
Berger du Nord Shetland (50-gram balls): 13 balls of No. 8771 black and 15 balls of No. 8753 teal
Size 10½ circular 36-inch-long knitting needle
Size H aluminum crochet hook
Yarn bobbins

Abbreviations: See page 77.
Gauge: With 2 strands of yarn held tog, 3 sts = 1 inch; 4 rows = 1 inch.

INSTRUCTIONS
Note: To facilitate alternating 2 strands of yarn, wind yarn onto bobbins for each check. For the first row of checks you will need 5 black bobbins and 11 teal bobbins. Carry ball of teal yarn across row as you work.

For the second row of checks you will need 6 teal bobbins and 11 black bobbins. Carry ball of black yarn across row as you work.

With 2 strands of teal held tog, cast on 132 sts.

FIRST BAND OF CHECKS: *Row 1:* With 2 strands of teal held together (1 with ball of teal, 1 with teal bobbin), k 12; * drop teal bobbin, pick up black bobbin. With ball of teal and black bobbin held tog, k 12; drop black bobbin, pick up teal bobbin. With ball of teal and teal bobbin held tog, k 12; rep from * 4 times more—6 teal checks and 5 teal/black checks begun.

Row 2: P across, working color changes as established in Row 1.

Rows 3–16: Rep rows 1 and 2 alternately; each check should be 4 inches square. Fasten off all yarn colors.

SECOND BAND OF CHECKS: *Row 17:* With 2 strands of yarn held tog (1 with ball of black, 1 with teal bobbin), k 12; * drop teal bobbin, pick up black bobbin. With ball of black and black bobbin held tog, k 12; drop black bobbin, pick up teal. With ball of black and teal bobbin, k 12; rep from * 4 times more—6 black/teal and 5 black checks begun.

Row 18: P across, working color changes with balls of yarn and bobbins as begun in Row 17.

Rows 19–32: Rep rows 17 and 18 alternately. Fasten off all yarn colors.

Rep First and Second Band of Checks until 15 bands are worked. Fasten off all colors.

EDGING: *Rnd 1:* With right side facing and crochet hook, join 2 strands of black held tog to bottom left-hand corner st, ch 1, in same st work sc, ch 2, sc; work sc evenly spaced around entire edge of afghan, working (sc, ch 2, sc) in each corner st; join to first sc, ch 1, turn.

Rnd 2: Sc in last sc made on previous rnd; sc in each sc around, working (sc, ch 2, sc) in each corner ch-2 sp; join to first sc; fasten off 1 strand of black; pick up 1 strand of teal. With teal and black held tog, ch 1, turn.

Rnds 3 and 4: With black and teal held tog, rep Rnd 2 of edging. At end of Rnd 4, drop black; pick up 1 strand of teal. With 2 strands of teal held tog, ch 1, turn.

Rnds 5 and 6: With 2 strands of teal held tog, rep Rnd 2 of edging. At end of Rnd 6, fasten off. Weave in all ends; block.

Crocheted Plaid Afghan

Shown on page 53.

Finished size is 48x59 inches.

MATERIALS
Unger Aries worsted yarn (3½-ounce balls): 10 balls of No. 415 blue (MC), 4 balls of No. 427 green (A), 3 balls of No. 456 camel (B), and 1 ball of No. 543 burgundy (C)
Size J aluminum crochet hook

Abbreviations: See page 73.
Gauge: 15 sts = 4 inches.

INSTRUCTIONS:
CENTER PANEL (make 2): With MC, ch 27.

Foundation row (wrong side): Sc in second ch from hook, ch 1, sk next ch (for stripe insert), sc in next ch; * ch 1, sk ch, sc in next ch; rep from * to within last 5 ch; ch 1, sk ch, sc in each of next 2 ch, ch 1, sk next ch (for stripe insert), sc in last ch; ch 1, turn.

Row 1 (right side): Sc in first sc, ch 1, sk next ch-1 sp, sc in next sc; * ch 1, sk sc, sc in next ch-1 sp; rep from * 9 times more; sc in next sc, ch 1, sk ch-1 sp, sc in last sc; ch 1, turn.

continued

Rows 2–24: Rep Row 1; at end of Row 24, do not ch 1; fasten off, turn.

Row 25 (right side): Join B in first sc, ch 1, sc in same st as join, ch 1, sk ch-1 sp, sc in *each* sc and ch-1 sp across to within last ch-1 sp; ch 1, sk ch-1 sp, sc in last sc; fasten off B, turn.

Row 26: Join MC in first sc, ch 1, sc in same as join; ch 1, sk ch-1 sp, sc in next sc, * ch 1, sk next sc, sc in next sc; rep from * 9 times more; sc in next sc, ch 1, sk ch-1 sp, sc in last sc; ch 1, turn.

Row 27: Rep Row 1; fasten off MC, turn.

Row 28: Join A in first sc, ch 1, rep Row 1; ch 2, turn.

Row 29: Dc in first sc, ch 1, sk ch-1 sp, dc in *each* sc and ch-1 sp to within last ch-1 sp; ch 1, sk ch-1 sp, dc in last sc, ch 1, turn.

Row 30: Sc in first dc, ch 1, sk next ch-1 sp, sc in next dc; * ch 1, sk dc, sc in next dc; rep from * 9 times more; sc in next dc, ch 1, sk ch-1 sp, sc in last dc; fasten off A; turn.

Row 31: Join MC in first sc, ch 1, rep Row 1; ch 1, turn.

Row 32: Rep Row 1; fasten off MC, turn.

Row 33: Join C in first sc, ch 1, rep Row 1; fasten off C, turn.

Rows 34–35: With MC, rep rows 31–32; fasten off MC, turn.

Rows 36–38: With A, rep rows 28–30; fasten off A at end of Row 38, turn.

Row 39: Join MC in first sc, ch 1, and rep Row 1; ch 1, turn.

Row 40: Rep Row 1; fasten off MC, turn.

Row 41: With B, rep Row 25; fasten off B, turn.

Row 42: With MC, rep Row 26, ch 1, turn.

Rep rows 1–42 three times more, then rep rows 1–24—5 blocks of MC completed; fasten off.

LEFT PANEL (make 1): With MC, ch 27.

Foundation row (wrong side): Sc in second ch from hook, * ch 1, sk ch, sc in next ch; rep from * to within last 5 ch; ch 1, sk ch, sc in each of next 2 ch, ch 1, sk ch for stripe insert, sc in last ch; ch 1, turn.

Row 1 (right side): Sc in first sc, ch 1, sk ch-1 sp, sc in next sc; * ch 1, sk sc, sc in next ch-1 sp; rep from * 10 times more; sc in last sc, ch 1, turn.

Row 2: Sc in first sc; * ch 1, sk sc, sc in next ch-1 sp; rep from * 10 times more; sc in next sc, ch 1, sk ch-1 sp, sc in last sc, ch 1, turn.

Rows 3–24: Rep rows 1 and 2 alternately; at end of Row 24, do not ch 1; fasten off, turn.

Row 25 (right side): Join B in first sc, ch 1, sc in same st as join; ch 1, sk ch-1 sp, sc in *each* sc and ch-1 sp across row; fasten off B, turn.

Row 26: Join MC in first sc, ch 1, sc in same st as join; * ch 1, sk sc, sc in next sc; rep from * 10 times more; sc in next sc; ch 1, sk ch-1 sp, sc in last sc; ch 1, turn.

Row 27: Rep Row 1 of Left Panel; fasten off MC, turn.

Row 28: Join A in first sc, ch 1, rep Row 2 of Left Panel; ch 2, turn.

Row 29: Dc in first sc, ch 1, sk ch-1 sp, dc in *each* sc and ch-1 sp across row; ch 1, turn.

Row 30: Sc in first dc; * ch 1, sk dc, sc in next dc; rep from * 10 times more; sc in next dc, ch 1, sk ch-1 lp, sc in last dc; fasten off A, turn.

Row 31: Join MC in first sc, ch 1; rep Row 1 of Left Panel; ch 1, turn.

Row 32: Rep Row 2 of Left Panel; fasten off MC, turn.

Row 33: Join C in first sc, ch 1; rep Row 1 of Left Panel; fasten off C, turn.

Row 34: Join MC in first sc, ch 1; rep Row 2 of Left Panel, ch 1, turn.

Row 35: Rep Row 1 of Left Panel; fasten off MC, turn.

Rows 36–38: With A, rep rows 28–30 of Left Panel; fasten off A at end of Row 38, turn.

Row 39: Join MC in first sc, ch 1; rep Row 1 of Left Panel, turn.

Row 40: Rep Row 2 of Left Panel; fasten off MC, turn.

Row 41: With B, rep Row 25 of Left Panel; fasten off B, turn.

Row 42: With MC, rep Row 26 of Left Panel, ch 1, turn.

Rep rows 1–42 three times more; then rep rows 1–24—5 MC blocks completed; fasten off.

RIGHT PANEL (make 1): With MC, ch 27.

Foundation row (wrong side): Sc in second ch from hook, ch 1, sk ch for stripe insert, sc in next ch; * ch 1, sk ch, sc in next ch; rep from * 10 times more, sc in last ch; ch 1, turn.

Row 1 (right side): Sc in first sc; * ch 1, sk sc, sc in next ch-1 sp; rep from * 10 times more; sc in next sc, ch 1, sk ch-1 sp, sc in last sc; ch 1, turn.

Row 2: Sc in first sc, ch 1, sk ch-1 sp, sc in next sc; * ch 1, sk sc, sc in next ch-1 sp; rep from * 10 times more, sc in last sc, ch 1, turn.

Rows 3–24: Rep rows 1 and 2 alternately; at end of Row 24, do not ch 1; fasten off, turn.

Row 25 (right side): Join B in first sc, ch 1, sc in same st as join; sc in *each* sc and ch-1 sp to within last ch-1 sp; ch 1, sk ch-1 sp, sc in last sc; fasten off B, turn.

Row 26: Join MC in first sc, ch 1, sc in same st as join; ch 1, sk next ch-1 sp, sc in next sc, * ch 1, sk sc, sc in next sc; rep from * 10 times more; sc in last sc; ch 1, turn.

Row 27: Rep Row 1 of Right Panel; fasten off MC, turn.

Row 28: Join A in first sc, ch 1; rep Row 2 of Right Panel; ch 2, turn.

Row 29: Dc in first sc and in *each* sc and ch-1 sp to within last ch-1 sp; ch 1, sk ch-1 sp, dc in last sc; ch 1, turn.

Row 30: Sc in first dc, ch 1, sk ch-1 sp, sc in next dc; * ch 1, sk dc, sc in next dc; rep from * 10 times more, sc in last dc; fasten off A, turn.

Row 31: Join MC in first sc, ch 1; rep Row 1 of Right Panel; ch 1, turn.

Row 32: Rep Row 2 of Right Panel; fasten off MC, turn.

Row 33: Join C in first sc, ch 1; rep Row 1 of Right Panel; fasten off C, turn.

Row 34: Join MC in first sc, ch 1; rep Row 2 of Right Panel; ch 1, turn.

Row 35: Rep Row 1 of Right Panel; fasten off MC, turn.

Rows 36–38: With A, rep rows 28–30 of Right Panel, fasten off A at end of Row 38, turn.

Row 39: Join MC in first sc, ch 1; rep Row 1 of Right Panel; ch 1, turn.

Row 40: Rep Row 2 of Right Panel; fasten off MC, turn.

Row 41: With B, rep Row 25 of Right Panel; fasten off B, turn.

Row 42: With MC, rep Row 26 of Right Panel; ch 1, turn.

Rep rows 1–42 three times more; rep rows 1–24—5 MC blocks completed; fasten off.

NARROW PANEL (Make 3): With MC, ch 8.

Foundation row: Sc in second ch from hook, ch 1, sk ch, sc in next ch; ch 1, sk ch for stripe insert, sc in next ch, ch 1, sk ch, sc in last ch; ch 1, turn.

Row 1 (right side): Sc in first sc, sc in next ch-1 sp, sc in next sc, ch 1, sk ch-1 sp, sc in next sc, sc in next ch-1 sp, sc in last sc; ch 1, turn.

Row 2 (wrong side): Sc in first sc, ch 1, sk sc, sc in next sc, ch 1, sk ch-1 sp, sc in next sc, ch 1, sk sc, sc in last sc; ch 1, turn.

Rows 3–24: Rep rows 1 and 2 alternately, at end of Row 24, do not ch 1; fasten off, turn.

Row 25 (right side): Join B in first sc, ch 1, sc in same st as join, sc in ch-1 sp, sc in next sc, ch 1, sp ch-1 sp, sc in next sc, sc in next ch-1 sp, sc in last sc; fasten off B, turn.

Row 26: Join MC in first sc, ch 1, sc in same st as join, ch 1, sk sc, sc in next sc, ch 1, sk ch-1 sp, sc in next sc, ch 1, sk sc, sc in last sc; ch 1, turn.

Row 27: Rep Row 1 of Narrow Panel; fasten off MC, turn.

Row 28: Join A in first sc, ch 1; rep Row 2 of Narrow Panel; ch 2, turn.

Row 29: Dc in first sc, dc in next ch-1 sp, dc in next sc, ch 1, sk ch-1 sp, dc in next sc, dc in next ch-1 sp, dc in last sc; ch 1, turn.

Row 30: Sc in first dc, ch 1, sk next dc, ch 1, sk ch-1 sp, sc in next dc, ch 1, sk dc, sc in last dc; fasten off A, turn.

Row 31: Join MC in first sc, ch 1; rep Row 1 of Narrow Panel; ch 1, turn.

Row 32: Rep Row 2 of Narrow Panel; fasten off MC, turn.

Row 33: Join C in first sc, ch 1; rep Row 1 of Narrow Panel; fasten off C, turn.

Row 34: Join MC in first sc, ch 1; rep Row 2 of Narrow Panel; ch 1, turn.

Row 35: Rep Row 1 of Narrow Panel; fasten off MC, turn.

Rows 36–38: With A, rep rows 28–30 of Narrow Panel; fasten off A at end of Row 38, turn.

Row 39: Join MC in first sc, ch 1; rep Row 1 of Narrow Panel; ch 1, turn.

Row 40: Rep Row 2 of Narrow Panel; fasten off MC, turn.

Row 41: With B, rep Row 25 of Narrow Panel; fasten off B, turn.

Row 42: With MC, rep Row 26 of Narrow Panel; ch 1, turn.

Rep rows 1–42 three times more; then rep rows 1–24—5 MC blocks completed; fasten off.

VERTICAL STRIPING

For the Two Center Panels

With 2 strands of B, work vertical stripe in ch-1 sps at *each* edge of Center Panels, working 1 ch in the ch-1 sps of sc rows and 2 chs in ch-1 sps of dc rows. Beginning at lower edge of panel, holding yarn beneath work, insert hook from front to back through the first ch-1 sp and pull up to front.

* Insert hook through next ch-1 sp (directly above), and draw up lp to front of work and pull through lp on hook; rep from * to top of afghan; drop lp from hook and with hook on underside of work, pull last lp through; fasten off.

For the Two Side Panels

Work vertical striping as for Center Panels with B.

For the Three Narrow Panels

Work vertical striping as for Center Panels with C.

CENTER AND SIDE PANEL EDGING: With right side facing and A, work 1 row in sc, ch-1 pat evenly spaced along *both* long edges of Center Panels and on the *inside* edges of the Right and Left panels. Begin and end each row with a sc; fasten off.

NARROW PANEL EDGING: *Row 1:* With A and wrong side of panel facing, work in sc, ch-1 pat evenly spaced along *both* long edges of all panels, beginning and ending row with a sc; ch 2, turn.

Row 2: Dc in *each* sc and ch-1 sp across row; fasten off.

Rep rows 1 and 2 on all long edges of Narrow Panels.

Pin 1 Narrow Panel between 2 Center Panels, matching lines and blocks and whipstitch together through *back lps* only.

Join 1 Narrow Panel between Center and 1 Side Panel and whipstitch together. Rep for other side.

BORDER: *Rnd 1:* With right side facing and MC, work 1 rnd of sc around entire afghan edge, working 3 sc in each corner; join to first sc.

Rnds 2–4: * Ch 3, work dc in each st around, working 5 dc in each corner st; join to top of ch-3; at end of Rnd 4, fasten off. Block.

Knitted Glen Plaid Afghan

Shown on pages 54 and 55.

Finished size is 47x59 inches, excluding fringe.

MATERIALS
Ulltex Worsted Match Yarn (50-gram balls): 16 skeins of No. 2622 purple; 10 skeins of No. 2662 gray; 2 skeins of No. 2644 white; and 1 skein *each* of No. 2626 rose, No. 2624 fuchsia, and No. 2600 green
Size 9 circular 36-inch-length knitting needle; stitch marker
Size 6 knitting needles
Size G aluminum crochet hook

Abbreviations: See page 77.
Gauge: 13 sts = 3 inches.

INSTRUCTIONS
The afghan is worked in rnds. Knit all sts (unless stated otherwise) and carry colors along the backside as you work. With purple, cast on 204 sts; join, taking care not to twist.
Rnd 1: P 3, k to end; place marker on needle.
Rnd 2: Purl.
Rnd 3: P 3 (hereafter always purl the first 3 sts of each round). *Working from Chart 1,* and reading from right to left, begin at A and work 17 sts to B; rep from C to B over 20 sts 9 times; work rem 4 sts from B to D.
Rnds 4–42: Continue to read chart from right to left until 2 repeats of Chart 1 are completed.
Rnd 43: P 3, *working from Chart 2* and reading from right to left, begin at A and work 12 sts to B 16 times; work last 9 sts from A to C.
Work 30 rnds of Chart 2; then repeat Chart 1 eight times more; work first 10 rnds of Chart 1.
Rep Chart 2, working in reverse (read chart from top to bottom).
Work Chart 1 for 2 complete repeats. Break off gray and with purple, p 1 rnd.
Last rnd: P 3, knit to end. Bind off loosely.

CHART 2

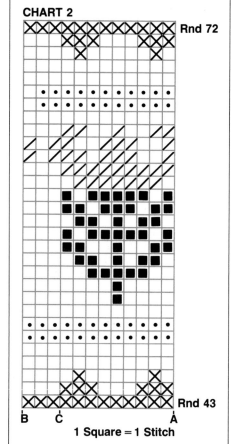

Rnd 72

Rnd 43

B   C   A

1 Square = 1 Stitch

COLOR KEY
⊠ Purple   ■ Green
⊡ Rose   ⧄ Fuchia
☐ White

FACINGS (make 2): With purple yarn, cast on 8 sts on Size 6 needles.
Row 1: Knit.
Row 2: P 6, k 2. Rep rows 1 and 2 until facing measures 2 inches less than length of afghan. Bind off. (Facings will stretch.)

FINISHING: With sewing machine and matching thread, sew zigzag stitches along purl ridge as close to *but not into first knit st.* Sew down the length of the afghan, turn, and rep atop these sts. Repeat zigzag stitching on

CHART 1

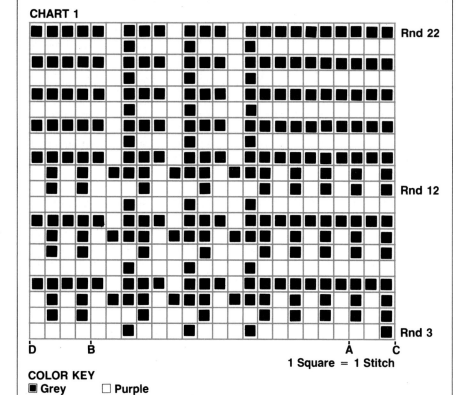

Rnd 22

Rnd 12

Rnd 3

D   B   A   C

1 Square = 1 Stitch

COLOR KEY
■ Grey   ☐ Purple

other side of the purl ridge. Cut afghan open between lines of machine stitching. Lay afghan flat, right side up. Lay facing, wrong side up, on top of machine stitching and sew in place over first knit st of afghan with back sts. Turn afghan over and fold facing to wrong side and whipstitch in place, taking care to cover all frayed edges and yarn ends. Repeat process on other edge. Steam afghan lightly.

FRINGE: * Cut 8 pieces of purple yarn 15 inches long. With crochet hook, fold all 8 strands in half and pull through 1 st along cast on edge and knot. Rep from * across, skipping 4 sts bet each tassel. Rep on bound off edge. Trim ends.

Knitted Argyle Afghan

Shown on page 56.

Finished size is 48x66 inches.

MATERIALS
Ulltex Match worsted yarn (50-gram balls): 16 balls of No. 2602 dark gray and 10 balls of No. 2652 gold
Size 10½ circular 36-inch knitting needle
Size 5 straight knitting needle

Abbreviations: See page 77.
Gauge: 4 sts = 1 inch; 18 rows = 4 inches.

INSTRUCTIONS
With dark gray and circular needle, cast on 201 sts, join, and work tubular throughout.
Rnd 1: Purl 3, knit to end, place marker.
Rnd 2 and all rnds thereafter: P 3; reading from right to left and carrying colors as you work, be-

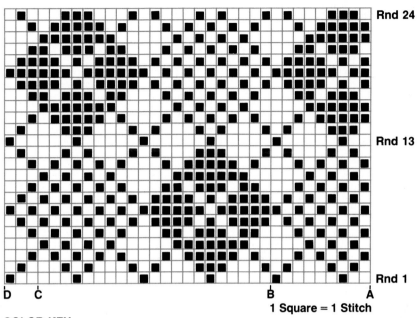

Rnd 24

Rnd 13

Rnd 1

D   C   B   A

1 Square = 1 Stitch

COLOR KEY
■ Gold   □ Dark grey

gin to work from chart, *above,* at A and k 33 sts to D; (k from B to D over 24 sts) 6 times; then k from B to C over 21 sts to complete rnd.
Continue to work from chart and always p 3 sts at beg of each rnd and k in pat across rem sts. Work chart through Rnd 24; then rep rnds 1–24 ten times more. Work rnds 1–13 to complete pat. Break off gold, k 1 rnd in gray, bind off loosely. Steam afghan lightly.
With sewing machine set for zigzag or overcast st, and working through 1 thickness only of afghan, sew along the length of the p ridge as closely as possible to the first k st on body of the afghan. At end, rotate work and stitch back atop same stitching. Rep steps on the other side of the p 3 ridge. Cut afghan apart between lines of machine stitching. Set afghan aside.

FACINGS (make 2): With gray and Size 5 needles, cast on 8 sts.
Row 1: Knit across.
Row 2: P 6, k 2. Rep rows 1 and 2 until facing measures 2 inches less than length of afghan. Bind off. (Facings will stretch.)

FINISHING: Lay afghan out right side up. Lay facing purl side up atop right edge of afghan, placing plain edge of facing just inside machine stitching and stretching to fit; backstitch in place. Steam seam and fold to wrong side of afghan. Whip garter stitch edge of facing to wrong side of afghan. Repeat finishing steps on left side of afghan.

FRINGE: Cut 560 strands of gray yarn, each 16 inches long. With wrong side of afghan facing and 4 strands of yarn held tog, fold yarn strands in half and with crochet hook pull through first st of cast on edge. Pull ends through loop and draw up tightly. Rep in every other st across cast on edge. Rep along bound-off edge. Steam entire afghan 1 more time.

Crocheted Argyle Afghan

Shown on page 57.

Finished size is 50x60 inches.

MATERIALS
Unger Aries worsted yarn (3½-ounce balls): 10 balls of No. 402 purple, 9 balls of No. 457 camel, and 2 balls of No. 543 burgundy
Size H aluminum crochet hook
Set of knitting bobbins

Abbreviations: See page 73.
Gauge: 7 dc = 2 inches; 4 dc rows = 2 inches.

INSTRUCTIONS
Note: Each diamond-shape area requires a separate bobbin. Before beginning, wind 10 bobbins with purple and 9 with camel. The burgundy crossbars are crocheted atop the surface after the afghan is completed.

TO CHANGE COLORS: Work to st before color change, with color in use, work dc to point where 2 lps rem on hook, drop color in use, pick up new color, yo, draw through 2 lps on hook. When working on the *right side* of work, drop bobbins to *wrong side* as you finish working with them.

With purple, ch 147 loosely.
Row 1 (right side): Dc in fourth ch from hook and in next 6 ch, changing to camel in last dc; * with camel, work 1 dc in next ch, finishing dc with purple; with purple, dc in next 15 ch, changing to camel in last dc; rep from * across to within last 9 sts; end with 1 dc with camel, changing to purple and 8 dc with purple; ch 3, turn.
Row 2: With purple, dc in second dc and each of next 5 dc, changing to camel in last dc—7 purple sts counting ch-3 as dc; *

with camel, dc in next 3 dc, changing to purple in last dc; with purple, dc in next 13 dc, changing to camel in last dc; rep from * across; end 3 dc with camel and 7 dc with purple; ch 3, turn.
Note: The purple half-diamonds at both sides of afghan will have color changes only on the inside edges. On instructions that follow, the 2 side diamonds will change color only once on each row.
Rows 3–8: Continue in rows of dc, working 1 *less* purple dc on each side of the center purple diamonds and 1 *more* camel dc on each side of the camel diamonds—at end of Row 8 there will be 15 dc in each center camel diamond, and 1 dc in purple between each camel diamond.
Rows 9–15: Continue in rows of dc, working 1 *less* camel dc on each side of the camel diamonds and 1 *more* purple dc on each side of the purple diamonds—at end of Row 15 there will be 15 dc in each center purple diamonds, 8 dc in each side purple half-diamonds, and 1 dc in camel between each purple diamond.
Rep rows 2–15 for pat until 7 camel diamonds in each strip along length of afghan are completed; fasten off all ends except last purple thread in use at upper left-hand corner.

BORDER: *Rnd 1:* With purple, work sc evenly spaced around all 4 sides of afghan, making 3 sc in each corner; join to first sc.
Rnd 2: With purple, sc in each sc around, working 3 sc in each corner sc; join with sl st to first sc; fasten off.
Working as for rnds 1 and 2 of border, work 2 rnds in camel, 2 rnds in burgundy, 2 rnds in purple; fasten off, tie in all ends.

CROSS-LINES: The burgundy cross-lines are worked diagonally across the diamonds, using surface slip stitches to look like embroidered chain stitches.
Make slip knot with burgundy, and hold burgundy yarn on wrong side of work. Starting at

lower right corner of afghan, in dc along edge of purple half-diamond, **insert hook from front to back and draw up burgundy lp to top side; with lp on hook, insert hook again from front to back in a diagonal direction (1 stitch up and 1 stitch over), pull up lp and draw through lp on hook—sl st ch made.** Continue in this way diagonally across center of diamonds to opposite side of afghan, taking care not to pull yarn too tightly; fasten off.
* Beg next cross-line in eighth st of next purple diamond and working from right to left, work sl st chs to opposite side; fasten off; rep from * across the bottom of the afghan.
Using the same dcs along bottom of afghan, work the diagonal lines that run across the afghan from left to right, taking care that cross-lines intersect in the center of the diamonds as you work across.

Fisherman Crocheted Afghan

Shown on page 59.

Finished size is 57x59 inches.

MATERIALS
Bernat Sesame No. 4 worsted yarn (100-gram balls): 3 balls of No. 7841 flax heather, 2 balls of No. 7862 ragg heather, and 14 balls of No. 7540 oyster
Size H crochet hook

Abbreviations: See page 73.
Gauge: 3 dc = 1 inch.

Instructions
Side Panels (make 2): Beg at lower edge, ch 47.
Row 1: Dc in fourth ch from hook and in each ch across—45 dc, counting turning ch as dc; ch 3, turn.
Note: On all right side (even-number) rows, work trc around post of dc *from the front.* Always sk the dc behind the trc that is worked around the post.

Row 2 (right side): Sk first 2 dc; trc around post of next dc, trc around post of *second* skipped dc; dc in next 2 dc; **(sk next 2 dc, trc around post of next dc; trc around post of second skipped dc; trc around post of first skipped dc) twice—2 raised cables made over 6 sts; dc in next 2 dc; sk next dc, trc around post of next dc, trc around post of skipped dc—raised cable over 2 dc made; dc in next 7 dc; work 4 dc in next dc, drop hook from work and insert hook in first dc *from front* of 4-dc grp, draw dropped lp through, ch 1—popcorn (pc) made on right side;** dc in next 7 dc; work raised cable over next 2 dc; dc in next 2 dc; work 2 raised cables over next 6 dc; dc in next 2 dc; work raised cable over next 2 dc; dc in turning ch-3 lp; ch 3, turn.

Note: On wrong side (odd-number) rows, work all trcs around posts of trc *from the back.* Always sk the st behind the raised trc.

Row 3 (wrong side): Sk first dc, [trc around posts of next 2 trc; dc in next 2 dc; trc around posts of next 6 trc; dc in next 2 dc, trc around posts of next 2 trc]; dc in next 6 sts; **(work 4 dc in next dc, drop hook from work, insert hook in first dc *from back* of 4-dc grp, draw the dropped lp through, ch 1—popcorn (pc) made on wrong side,** dc in next st) twice; dc in next 5 dc; rep bet [ ]s once; dc in turning ch-3 lp; ch 3, turn.

Row 4: **Sk first dc and next trc; trc around post of next trc, trc around post of skipped trc—beg-cable made;** dc in next 2 dc, work 2 raised cables around posts of next 6 trc; dc in next 2 dc; make raised cable around posts of next 2 trc; dc in next 5 sts; (pc in next dc, dc in next st) 3 times; dc in next 4 dc, make raised cable around posts of next 2 trc; dc in next 2 dc; make 2 raised cables around posts of next 6 trc; dc in next 2 dc; make raised cable around posts of next 2 trc; dc in turning ch-3 lp; ch 3, turn.

Row 5: Rep bet [ ]s of Row 3; then dc in next 4 sts; (pc in next dc, dc in next st) 4 times; dc in next 3 sts; rep bet [ ]s of Row 3; dc in turning ch-3 lp; ch 3, turn.

Row 6: Work beg cable around post of next 2 trc; dc in next 2 dc; make 2 raised cables around posts of next 6 trc; dc in next 2 dc, make raised cable around posts of next 2 trc; dc in next 3 dc; (pc in next dc, dc in next st) 5 times; dc in next 2 dc; raised cable around posts of next 2 trc; dc in next 2 dc; make 2 raised cables around post of next 6 trc; dc in next 2 dc, raised cable around posts of next 2 trc; dc in turning ch-3 lp; ch 3, turn.

Row 7: Rep Row 5.
Row 8: Rep Row 4.
Row 9: Rep Row 3.
Row 10: Work beg cable around posts of next 2 trc; dc in next 2 dc; make 2 raised cables around post of next 6 trc; dc in next 2 dc; make raised cable around post of next 2 trc; dc in next 7 sts, pc in next dc, dc in next 7 sts; raised cable around posts of next 2 trc; dc in next 2 dc; 2 raised cables around posts of next 6 trc; dc in next 2 dc; raised cable around posts of next 2 trc; dc in turning ch-3 lp; ch 3, turn.

Row 11: Rep bet [ ]s of Row 3; dc in next 15 sts; rep bet [ ]s of Row 3; dc in turning ch-3 lp; ch 3, turn.

Row 12: Rep Row 10.
Rep rows 3–12 for pat 10 times more. On last repeat, end with Row 11; fasten off.

INSIDE BORDER FOR LEFT SIDE PANEL: *Row 1:* With right side facing, join oyster yarn in bottom right-hand corner around turning-ch, ch 1. Working along long edge of panel, work 1 sc in same turning-lp; * 2 sc in next turning-lp, 1 sc in next turning-lp; rep from * to opposite end of strip, ch 1, turn.

Row 2 (wrong side): Sc in first sc, * **insert hook in next sc and draw up a lp; working chs through first lp on hook, ch 3, yo, draw through 2 lps on hook, pushing bead to right side of work, sc in next sc—bead st over 2 sts made;** rep from * across row, ending sc in last sc; fasten off, turn.

Row 3: With right side facing, join flax heather in first sc, ch 1, sc in same st and each st across, ch 1, turn.

Row 4: Sc in first 2 sc, * work bead st over next 2 sts, rep from * across, ending sc in last 2 sc; fasten off.

Rows 5 and 6: With oyster, rep rows 1 and 2; fasten off.

Rows 7 and 8: With ragg heather, rep rows 3 and 4; fasten off.

Rows 9 and 10: With oyster, rep rows 1 and 2; fasten off.

Rows 11 and 12: With flax heather, rep rows 3 and 4; fasten off.

Rows 13 and 14: With oyster, rep rows 1 and 2; do not fasten off; ch 2, turn.

Row 15: Sk first sc, hdc in next sc, * ch 1, sk next sc, hdc in next sc; rep from * across row to last 2 sc; end hdc in last 2 sc; ch 1, turn.

Row 16: Sc in each of first 2 hdc, * sc in next ch-1 sp; 2 sc in next ch-1 sp; rep from * across; end sc in last hdc and top of ch-2; fasten off.

INSIDE BORDER FOR RIGHT SIDE PANEL: With right side facing, join oyster yarn in top left corner around turning ch-lp and work as for rows 1–16 of Border for Left Side Panel.

CENTER PANEL: Beg at bottom edge, ch 63.
Note: Always work trc around posts *from the front.*
Row 1 (wrong side): Dc in fourth ch from hook and in each ch across—61 dc counting turning ch as dc; ch 2, turn.

Row 2 (right side): Sk first dc, dc around posts *from front* of next 2 dc, dc in next 2 dc, * sk next 2 dc, **trc around post from *front* of next dc—raised trc slanting to the right;** dc in *second* skipped dc, **trc around post of *first* skipped dc—raised trc slanting to the left;** dc in next unworked dc and next 4 dc, rep from * 6 times more until 3 sts rem; dc around posts from front of next 2 dc, hdc in top of turning ch; ch 3, turn.

continued

Row 3 and all odd-number rows: Sk first dc, dc in each st across and top of ch-2; ch 2, turn.

Row 4: Sk first dc, dc around posts of next 2 dc, dc in next dc; * trc around post of raised trc slanting to the right 2 rows below, sk next dc, dc in next 3 dc; trc around post of raised trc slanting to the left 2 rows below, sk dc, dc in next 3 dc; rep from * 6 times more until 3 sts rem, dc around posts of next 2 dc, hdc in top of ch-3; ch 3, turn.

Row 6: Sk first dc, dc around posts of next 2 dc, * trc around post of raised trc 2 rows below, sk dc, dc in next 5 dc, trc around posts of raised trc 2 rows below, sk dc, dc in next dc; rep from * 6 times more until 4 sts rem; sk dc, dc around posts of next 2 dc, hdc in top of ch-3; ch 3, turn.

Row 8: Sk first dc, dc around posts of next 2 dc, trc around post of raised trc 2 rows below, * sk dc, dc in next 5 dc, sk next raised trc, trc around post of trc slanting to the right, sk dc, dc in next dc, trc around post of skipped raised trc slanting to left; rep from * 5 times more; sk next dc, dc in next 5 dc, trc around post of raised trc 2 rows below, sk dc, dc around posts of next 2 dc, hdc in top of ch-3; ch 3, turn.

Row 10: Sk first dc, dc around posts of next 2 dc, trc around post of raised trc 2 rows below; * sk dc, dc in next 3 dc, trc around post of raised trc slanting to the right 2 rows below, sk dc, dc in next 3 dc, trc around post of raised trc slanting to left; rep from * 5 times more; sk dc, dc in next 3 dc, trc around post of raised trc 2 rows below, sk dc, dc in next 2 dc; dc around posts of next 2 dc, hdc in top of ch-2; ch 3, turn.

Row 12: Sk first dc, dc around posts of next 2 dc, dc in next 2 dc; * trc around post of raised trc 2 rows below, sk dc, dc in next dc, trc around post of raised trc 2 rows below, sk dc, dc in next 5 dc; rep from * 5 times more; trc around post of raised trc 2 rows below, sk dc, dc in next dc, trc around post of raised trc 2 rows below, sk dc, dc in next 2 dc, dc around posts of next 2 dc, hdc in top of ch-2; ch 3, turn.

Row 14: Sk first dc, dc around posts of next 2 dc, dc in next 2 dc; * sk next 2 dc, trc around post of raised trc slanting to the *right* 2 rows below, dc in second skipped dc, trc around post of raised trc just skipped and slanting to the left; sk dc, dc in next 5 dc, rep from * 5 times more; sk next 2 dc, trc around post of raised trc slanting to the right, dc in second skipped dc, trc around post of raised trc just skipped, sk dc, dc in next 2 dc, dc around posts of next 2 dc, hdc in top of turning ch; ch 3, turn.

Rep rows 3–14 for pattern and work until panel is same length as 2 side panels; fasten off.

With oyster yarn, pin and then whipstitch the side panels to the center panel.

BORDER: *Rnd 1:* With right side facing, join oyster yarn in top right-hand corner, ch 1, sc in same st as join. Working across the top edge of first panel, * **draw up lp in each of the next 2 sts, yo, draw through 3 lps on hook—dec made;** sc in next sc; rep from * to the striped panel; work 12 sc evenly spaced across the striped panel; work 54 sc across the center panel, working decs over every seventh and eighth st; complete left top edge to correspond to right side; work 2 more sc in corner st; working along left side edge, work from * of Row 1 for the Inside Border for Left Side Panel to the next corner. Work 2 more sc in corner st, then work rem 2 sides to correspond; end 2 sc in same st as first sc at beg of rnd; join to first sc; ch 1, turn.

Rnd 2: Rep as for Row 2 of Left Side Panel, working around the entire afghan; join to first sc; fasten off; turn.

Rnds 3–6: With flax heather, work as for rows 3 and 4 of Left Side Panel. *Note:* Only work the 3 sc in the corners on the odd-number rows. To stagger the bead sts, examine your work at the beg of

each new side and work 2 sc consecutively to establish the bead st pattern; join at end of each rnd; ch 1, turn. At end of Rnd 6, fasten off.

Working in pat as established, work 2 more rnds with oyster; fasten off; then 2 rnds with ragg heather; fasten off.

Fisherman Knit Afghan

28 · 50 gr.
Zellers
Sayelle
blue

Shown on page 58.

Finished size is 52x64 inches, excluding fringe.

MATERIALS
Unger Roly Poly (3½-ounce ball): 13 balls of No. 124 blue-green heather
Size 8 knitting needles
Size G aluminum crochet hook
Cable needle
Stitch markers

Abbreviations: See page 77.
Gauge: Width of panel A is 9½ inches; panel B is 8½ inches; panel C is 16 inches.

INSTRUCTIONS
SEED STITCH (worked over 6 sts)

Row 1 (right side): * K 1, p 1; rep from * twice more.

Row 2: K the p sts and p the k sts as they face you.

Rep these 2 rows for pat.

PLAIT CABLE (worked over 9 sts)

Row 1 (right side): Knit.

Row 2 and all even-number rows: Purl.

Rows 3, 7, and 9: Knit.

Row 5: K 3, sl next 3 sts to cable needle and hold in *front* of work, k next 3 sts from LH needle, k 3 from cable needle.

Row 11: Sl next 3 sts to cable needle and hold in *back* of work, k next 3 sts from LH needle, k 3 sts from cable needle, k 3.

Rep rows 1–12 for pat.

TRINITY STITCH (worked over 26 sts)

Row 1 (right side): Purl.

Row 2: K 1, * (k 1, p 1, k 1) all in next st; p 3 tog; rep from * 5 times more, k 1.

Row 3: Purl.

Row 4: K 1, * p 3 tog, (k 1, p 1, k 1) all in next st; rep from * 5 times more, k 1.

Rep rows 1–4 for pat.

HORSESHOE CABLE (worked over 9 sts)

Row 1 (right side): Knit.

Rows 2 and 4: Purl.

Row 3: Sl 3 sts to cable needle and hold in *back* of work, k 1, k 3 from cable needle, k 1, sl 1 to cable needle and hold in *front* of work, k 3, k 1 from cable needle.

Rep rows 1–4 for pat.

MOSS STITCH—DIAMOND PATTERN (worked over 28 sts)

Row 1 (right side): P 1, (p 5, k 1, p 1, k 1, p 5) twice, p 1.

Row 2 and all even-number rows: K the k sts and p the p sts as they face you.

Row 3: P 1, (p 4, **sl next st to cable needle and hold in back of work, k 1, p 1 from cable needle—right twist (RT) completed;** k 1, **sl next st to cable needle and hold in front of work, p 1, k 1 from cable needle—left twist (LT) completed;** p 4) twice, p 1.

Row 5: P 1, (p 3, RT, k 1, p 1, k 1, LT, p 3) twice, p 1.

Row 7: P 1, * p 2, RT, (k 1, p 1) twice; k 1, LT, p 2; rep from * once, p 1.

Row 9: P 1, * p 1, RT, (k 1, p 1) 3 times, k 1, LT, p 1; rep from * once, p 1.

Row 11: P 1, * RT, (k 1, p 1) 4 times, k 1, LT; rep from * once, p 1.

Row 13: P 1, * LT, (k 1, p 1) 4 times, p 1, RT; rep from * once, p 1.

Row 15: P 1, * p 1, LT (p 1, k 1) 3 times; p 1, RT, p 1; rep from * once, p 1.

Row 17: P 1, * p 2, LT, (p 1, k 1) twice, p 1, RT, p 2; rep from * once, p 1.

Row 19: P 1, * p 3, LT, p 1, k 1, p 1, RT, p 3; rep from * once, p 1.

Row 21: P 1, (p 4, LT, p 1, RT, p 4) twice, p 1.

Row 23: P 1, (p 5, **sl next 2 sts to cable needle and hold in back of work, k 1, sl p st st from cable needle to left needle and p it, k 1 from cable needle—double twist made,** p 5) twice, p 1.

Rep rows 3–24 for pat.

HONEYCOMB PATTERN (worked over 38 sts)

Row 1 (right side): P 3 (k 2, p 4) 5 times, k 2, p 3.

Row 2 and all even-number rows: K the k sts and p the p sts as they face you.

Row 3: P 1, (**sl 2 sts to cable needle and hold in back of work, k 1, p 2 from cable needle—back twist (BT) made; sl next st to cable needle and hold in front of work, p next 2 sts, k 1 from cable needle—front twist (FT) made**) 6 times, p 1.

Row 5: P 1, k 1, (p 4, k 2) 5 times, p 4, k 1, p 1.

Row 7: P 1, (FT, BT) 6 times, p 1.

Rep rows 1–8 for pat.

CENTER PLAIT CABLE (worked over 13 sts)

Row 1 (right side): K 1, p 1, k 9, p 1, k 1.

Row 2 and all even-number rows: K the k sts and p the p sts as they face you.

Rows 3, 5, 9, and 11: Rep Row 1.

Row 7: K 1, p 1, k 3, sl next 3 sts to cable needle and hold in *front* of work, k next 3 sts, k 3 from cable needle, p 1, k 1.

Row 13: K 1, p 1, sl next 3 sts to cable needle and hold in *back* of work, k next 3 sts, k 3 sts from cable needle, k 3, p 1, k 1.

Rep rows 2–13 for pat.

RIGHT SIDE PANEL: Cast on 47 sts. Work Row 1 of Seed Stitch pat over first 6 sts, place marker; work Row 1 of Plait Cable over next 9 sts, place marker; work Row 1 of Trinity Stitch pat over next 26 sts, place marker; work Row 1 of Seed Stitch pat over last 6 sts. Slipping markers as you work, continue in pats as established and work until length measures 64 inches; end with a wrong-side row. Bind off.

LEFT SIDE PANEL: Cast on 47 sts. Work Row 1 of Seed Stitch pat over first 6 sts, place marker; work Row 1 of Trinity Stitch pat over next 26 sts, place marker; work Row 1 of Plait Cable pat over next 9 sts, place marker; work Row 1 of Seed Stitch pat over last 6 sts. Slipping markers as you work, continue in pats as established and work until length measures 64 inches; end with a wrong-side row. Bind off.

INSIDE PANEL (make 2): Cast on 48 sts. P 1, place marker; work Row 1 of Horseshoe Cable over next 9 sts, place marker; work Row 1 of Moss-Diamond pat over next 28 sts, place marker; work Row 1 of Horseshoe Cable over next 9 sts, place marker, p 1. Purl first and last st of each right-side row and knit first and last st of each wrong-side row. Slipping markers as you work, continue in pats as established above, working until length measures 64 inches; ending with a wrong-side row. Bind off.

CENTER PANEL: Cast on 89 sts. Work Row 1 of Honeycomb pat over first 38 sts, place marker; work Row 1 of Center Plait Cable pat over next 13 sts, place marker; work Row 1 of Honeycomb pat over last 38 sts. Slipping markers as you work, continue in pats as established, working until length measures 64 inches; end with a wrong-side row. Bind off.

ASSEMBLY: Whipstitch 1 Inside Panel to each side of Center Panel; join Right Panel to right edge of 3 joined panels; join Left Panel to left edge of 4 joined panels. Work 1 row sc evenly spaced on 2 shorter ends.

FRINGE: Cut strands of yarn 10 inches long. Knot 2 strands in every st on short ends of afghan.

pillow 80 sts

STITCHER'S NOTEBOOK

CROCHETING PRIMER

Working a Foundation Chain

1 **Slip knot:** The slip knot is always the first loop on the hook. With the short end of the yarn lying across your left hand, loop the yarn into a pretzel shape, as shown *above*. Then insert the hook over the top of the outside strand on the right and *under* the next strand. Pull on both tails to tighten the loop on the hook.

2 **Holding the yarn in the left hand:** Using the strand coming from the ball of yarn and your right hand (still holding the slip knot on the hook), wrap the yarn completely around the little finger of your left hand, and carry it across the back of the three middle fingers. Allow the yarn to slide across the tip of your index finger as you work.

3 **Holding the hook in the right hand:** Hold the hook, with the slip knot on it, in your right hand as though you were holding a piece of chalk. With the tips of the thumb and middle finger of your left hand, hold the knot below the slip knot, as shown *above*.

Single Crochet

1 Ch 20; referring to photo 1, * insert hook from front to back under the top 2 loops of the *second* chain from the hook. Wrap yarn over the hook, and draw strand through the chain stitch only—2 loops on hook. Referring to photo 2, wrap yarn around hook and draw strand through both loops on the hook—1 single crochet made.

2 Working in *each* chain across the row (do not skip any chains), repeat from the * until all chains are worked—19 single crochets made. Then chain 1, and, without removing the hook from the work, turn the work over to begin the next row.

3 Notice the chains running across the top of each single crochet as you work the first row of stitches. These chains are the top 2 loops you will work *under* on the next row. After you turn your work, these chains are not visible. However, when you insert your hook in the tiny holes that appear below the top of the stitch as shown in photo *above*, you will slip your hook under the top 2 strands of the stitch.

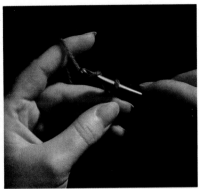

4 Making a chain: * With the hook lying across the front of the yarn strand leading to your index finger, wrap the yarn around the hook (yo) and pull the strand through the loop on the hook—1 chain made. Repeat from the * 19 times more—20 chains made. When working a foundation chain, the slip knot *never* counts as a chain stitch.

5 Working in the chains: Hold the strand of chains with your left hand so the *flat* side of the chains faces you. Three strands of yarn make up each chain. When working the first row of stitches in the strand of chains, unless stated otherwise, always work under the *two* top strands (loops) of the chain (or any stitch), as shown *above.*

Stitching in the Foundation Chain

As you begin the first row of crocheting, it's necessary to begin working in the appropriate chain to establish the first stitch in a row. When beginning a row of single crochet after completing the foundation chain, work the first single crochet in the *second* chain from the hook; work a half-double crochet in the *third* chain, a double crochet in the *fourth* chain, and a triple crochet in the *fifth* chain. In every instance *except* the single crochet, the chains preceding the first stitch count as the first stitch in the row.

To begin the second row, skip the chain-1 turning stitch and work a single crochet in the first single crochet as the work now faces you. Work a single crochet in each single crochet across the row—19 single crochets made; then chain 1, turn. To make a practice swatch, continue to work single crochets in each single crochet across and chain 1 at the end of each row before turning to begin a new row.

Abbreviations

beg	begin(ning)	rem	remaining
bl	block	rep	repeat
CC	contrasting color	RH	right hand
ch	chain	rnd	round
cl	cluster	sc	single crochet
dc	double crochet	sk	skip
dec	decrease	sl st	slip stitch
dtr	double treble crochet	sp	space
grp	group	st(s)	stitch(es)
hdc	half-double crochet	tog	together
inc	increase	trc	treble crochet
LH	left hand	yo	yarn over
lp(s)	loop(s)	*	repeat from * as indicated
MC	main color	( )	repeat between ( )s as indicated
pat	pattern	[ ]	repeat between [ ]s as indicated
pc	popcorn		

STITCHER'S NOTEBOOK

CROCHETING PRIMER

Half-Double Crochet

1 Working on the same swatch as already established, complete a row of single crochets; then chain 2 and turn work. This chain-2 will now count as the first stitch of the row.
   * Referring to photo 1, wrap yarn over hook, and insert hook into the *second* single crochet of the row below (under 2 top loops). *Note:* The photo shows the stitch step in the *fifth* single crochet; the preceding four stitches are made.

2 Wrap yarn over hook (photo 2), and draw strand through the single crochet stitch only—3 loops on hook. Wrap yarn over hook (photo 3), and draw strand through all 3 loops on hook—1 half-double crochet made. Working in *each* single crochet in the row (do not skip any stitches), repeat from the * across the row—18 half-double crochets made, plus the turning chain-2 at beginning of row. Chain 2, turn work.

3 To begin working the second row of half-double crochets, skip the first half-double crochet as the work now faces you, and repeat from the * across the row, working half-double crochets in top of each half-double crochet; work the last half-double crochet in the top of the chain-2 at the beginning of the previous row (work in the 2 top loops of the chain to avoid a hole in your work); then chain 2, turn.

Double Crochet

1 Working on the same swatch, complete a row of half-double crochets, then chain 3 and turn work. This chain-3 will count as the first stitch of the next row. * Referring to photo 1, wrap yarn over hook, and insert hook in the *second* half-double crochet of the row below (under 2 top loops), wrap yarn over hook (photo 2), and draw strand through the half-double crochet stitch only—3 loops on hook.

2 Wrap yarn over hook (photo 3), and draw strand through 2 loops—2 loops remain on hook; wrap yarn over hook, and draw strand through remaining 2 loops (photo 4)—1 double crochet made. Working in *each* half-double crochet across the row (do not skip any stitches), repeat from * across the row—18 double crochets made, plus the turning chain-3 at beginning of row; then chain 3, and turn work.

3 To begin working the second row of double crochets, skip the first double crochet as the work now faces you, and repeat from the * across the row, working a double crochet in top of each double crochet. Work the last double crochet in top of the chain-3 at the beginning of the previous row (work in the 2 top loops of the chain to avoid a hole in your work); then chain 3 and turn work.

Treble Crochet

1 Working on the same swatch, complete a row of double crochets; chain 4 and turn work. This chain-4 will count as the first stitch of the row. * Referring to photo 1, wrap yarn over hook *2 times,* and insert hook in the second double crochet of the row below (under 2 top loops). Wrap yarn over hook (photo 2), and draw strand through the double crochet stitch only—4 loops are now on hook.

2 Wrap yarn over hook (photo 3), and draw strand through 2 loops on hook—3 loops remain on hook; wrap yarn over hook and draw strand through 2 loops on hook—2 loops on hook; wrap yarn over hook and draw strand through last 2 loops on hook—1 treble crochet made.

Repeat from the * across the row, working one treble crochet in top of each double crochet—18 treble crochets made, plus the

3 turning chain at the beginning of the row; then chain 4 and turn work.

To begin working the second row of treble crochets, skip the first treble crochet as the work now faces you, and repeat from the * across the row, working a treble crochet in top of each treble crochet. Work the last treble crochet in top of the chain-4 at beginning of the previous row; then chain 4 and turn work.

4 Continue to work double crochets in each double crochet across the row to work the practice swatch and work chain-3 at end of each row before turning to begin a new row.

Slip Stitch

A slip stitch is used as a joining stitch when working in rounds, or to bind edges at the beginning of a row. It is frequently used in knitting to finish neckline and sleeve edges.

Working on the swatch as already established, complete a row of treble crochet, then chain 1 and turn work. * Insert hook in the first treble crochet, wrap yarn over hook (photo 1), and draw strand through the treble crochet and the loop on the hook—1 slip stitch made. Working in each treble crochet, repeat from the * across the row.

Fastening Off

At end of row, snip yarn, leaving a 6-inch tail. Wrap yarn over hook and draw the cut end through the loop on the hook. This last step knots the last stitch, and the work will not unravel. Weave the cut strand into the back of the finished work. The words "end off" and "break off" are synonymous with "fasten off"—all terms that mean you are finished working with the thread or yarn at this point in your work.

STITCHER'S NOTEBOOK

KNITTING PRIMER

Casting on with 2 strands of yarn

1 **Slip knot:** The slip knot is always the first loop on the right-hand needle and *counts as the first stitch on the row*. With the short end of the yarn lying across your left hand, make the pretzel-shape loop shown *above*. Then insert the needle over the top of the outside strand on the right and *under* the next strand. Pull on both tails to tighten the loop on the needle.

2 **Holding the yarn in the left hand:** Allowing approximately 1 inch of yarn for each stitch to be cast on, make a slip knot 20 inches from the end of the yarn to cast on 20 stitches. There are two strands of yarn coming from the needle. Referring to photo 2, wrap the *short* end around the left thumb and hold the remaining tail in place with the three back fingers of the left palm.

3 Temporarily holding the needle with the slip knot in your left hand, wrap the yarn coming from the ball of yarn in your right hand, as shown in photo 3. Then return the needle to your right hand to begin casting on.

Knitting

1 Begin to work with 2 needles, holding the needle with the cast-on stitches in your left hand. * With the yarn behind the work, insert the right needle *from the front* through the center of the first stitch on the left needle, as shown in photo 1.

2 Wrap the yarn in your right hand around the back and across the front of the right-hand needle as shown in photo, *above*.

3 Slide the right-hand needle toward yourself, and at the same time, tilt this needle and draw the wrapped strand of yarn through the loop on the left needle, as shown in photo 3.

4 * With the yarn behind the needle, drop the needle in your right hand toward the palm of your left hand. Referring to photo 4, insert the tip of the needle from front of work to back through the loop formed by the strand that is wrapped around your thumb.

5 Referring to photo 5, wrap the yarn in your right hand around the needle.

6 Slip the thumb loop over the needle, as shown in photo 6, and let it slide from your thumb. Draw up the loop to fit the needle.

Wrap the short strand of yarn around the thumb again and repeat from * 18 times more—20 stitches on the needle.

4 With the index finger of your left hand, slip the first loop off the left needle as shown in photo 4 and drop it from the needle—1 knit stitch made. Repeat from the * in each of the stitches across the row. Then transfer the right-hand needle to your left hand and begin a new row.

Abbreviations

beg .... begin(ning)	rep .... repeat
CC .... contrasting color	rnd .... round
dec .... decrease	sc .... single crochet
dp .... double point	sk .... skip
inc .... increase	sl st .... slip stitch
k .... knit	sp .... space
LH ....left hand	st(s) .... stitch(es)
lp(s) .... loop(s)	st st .... stockinette stitch
MC .... main color	tbl .... through back loop
p .... purl	tog .... together
pat .... pattern	yo .... yarn over
psso .... pass slip st over	* .... repeat from * as indicated
rem .... remaining	( ) repeat between ( )s as indicated
RH ....right hand	[ ] repeat between [ ]s as indicated

KNITTING PRIMER

Purling

1 Hold the needle with the stitches in your left hand.
* With the yarn in *front* of the work, and referring to the photo, *above,* insert the right needle *from the back* through the center of the first loop on the hook.

2 Wrap the yarn in your right hand, around the back and across the front of the right needle, as shown in photo 2.
  Slide the right needle toward yourself, and at the same time, catch the wrapped strand and "push" the strand through the loop on the left needle.

3 With the index finger of your left hand, slip the first loop from the left needle and drop from needle—1 purl stitch made.
  Repeat from the * in each of the stitches across the row. Then transfer the right-hand needle to the left hand and begin a new row of stitching.

Binding Off

1 After you complete the number of rows required in your knitting, you need to "bind off" these stitches to remove them from the needles.
  Knit (or purl) the first two stitches. Then, referring to the photo, *above,* insert the tip of the left needle into the first stitch on the right needle, lift over the second stitch, and drop from the needle—1 stitch bound off.

* Knit (or purl) the next stitch on the left needle, then lift the first stitch over the second stitch and drop from needle. Repeat from the * across the row until one stitch remains on the right needle. Cut the yarn, leaving a 6-inch tail, and pull up a loop with the right needle until yarn passes through the center of the last stitch. To avoid a lumpy knot, do not pull the end of yarn through the last loop on the needle.
  When you are working on a knit side, bind off stitches as if to knit; when working on a purl side, bind off stitches as if to purl. When binding off ribbing stitches, knit the knit stitches, and purl the purl stitches.

Increasing Stitches

When you add stitches to your knitting, the piece becomes wider. Increases are used to shape the work or to create pattern textures. There are any number of ways to work increases into your work and they'll all affect the finished appearance of your knitting. The three most common ways to work increases and their effects on your knitting follow.

Knitting or purling into the same stitch twice
  This technique for increasing is the most frequently used, but it produces a small *ridge* on the surface of the work when knitting in stockinette stitch. It is best to use this method when increasing on the *edges* of your work.
  When working an increase by *knitting* into the same stitch twice, knit the stitch as usual

from the front of the stitch, but do not drop the stitch from the left needle. Increase by inserting the tip of the right needle into the back loop of the same stitch (from front to back). Wrap the yarn around the right needle and draw the yarn through the back of the stitch. Then proceed to drop the stitch from the left needle.

To work an increase by *purling* into the same stitch twice, purl the stitch as usual, but do not remove the stitch from the left needle. Take the tip of the right needle around to the back of the left needle and insert the tip in the left side of the back loop; then bring it to the front of the work. Wrap the yarn around the right needle as for a regular purl stitch and complete the stitch. Drop the stitch from the left needle.

Yarn-over increases

Yarn-over increases are often found on raglan sleeve shapings, lacy patterns, and beadings on booties and other edges to run cord or ribbons through and are worked as follows:

When working an increase between two *knit stitches* by wrapping the yarn around the hook (yo), bring the yarn to the front of the work and wrap it counter-clockwise around the front of the right needle and return to the back of the work. Then knit the next stitch on the left needle. This method produces a small hole below the stitch.

To work an increase between two *purl stitches* when wrapping the yarn around the hook (yo), take the yarn completely around the right needle counterclock-wise, and return to the front. Then purl the next stitch.

Increasing in the running strand

This method of increasing is the least noticeable of any increase when working garments and works best when knitting in stockinette stitch.

When working on the knit side, work up to the point where the

increase is made. Insert the tip of the right needle, from the back, into the running loop before the next stitch and place the loop on the left needle. Then knit into the back of this loop.

On the purl side, work up to the point where the increase is made. Insert the tip of the right needle, from the front, into the running strand before the next stitch and place the loop on the left needle. Then purl the loop as you normally would.

In both of these methods, the finished stitch will appear twisted. This twist is necessay to avoid a hole in the succeeding row.

Decreasing Stitches

Your knitted piece becomes narrower when you decrease. Like increases, decreases are used to shape your knitting and affect pattern knitting. The most common methods of making decreases follow.

Working two stitches together

The simplest way to work a decrease is to knit or purl 2 stitches together. When decreasing *knitwise,* the resulting stitch will slant to the right: Insert the tip of the right needle into the front of the *second* stitch, then into the first stitch on the left needle. Wrap the yarn around the right needle and draw the strand through both stitches on the left needle and complete the stitch.

When decreasing *purlwise,* insert the tip of the right needle through the first, then through the second stitch on the left needle. Wrap yarn around the right needle and draw the strand through both stitches and complete the stitch.

Pass the slip stitch over

A method of decreasing that's similar to binding off is to slip 1, knit 1, and pass the slip stitch over the knit stitch. It is written

"sl 1, k 1, psso" or "skp." Work up to the point for the decrease, then insert the right needle into the next stitch on the left needle as though to knit and slip to right needle (do not knit it). Knit the next stitch. With tip of left needle, lift the slipped stitch over the knit stitch and drop from needle.

This method of decreasing is almost always worked on the knit side of the work and the resulting stitch will slant to the left.

To slip a stitch

A slip stitch is an unworked stitch and simply means to transfer a stitch from one needle to another without working it: Insert the right needle into the stitch on the left needle from the back, as if to purl. Then slip the stitch onto the right needle without working or twisting it. Always slip a stitch *purlwise* unless directions cite otherwise or when working the sl 1, k 1, psso decrease.

When working on the *knit* side, do *not* bring the yarn forward to slip the stitch *unless* the instructions indicate otherwise.

When working on the *purl* side, keep yarn at the front when slipping the next stitch (do not take the yarn to the back of the work).

Changing Needles

Instructions frequently require changing needles from one size to another on the same piece of knitting. For example, when working a sweater, the ribbing portions at hip, neckline, and sleeves may be worked with a smaller-size needle than the remaining portions of the sweater. Two rows of knitting are required to change needles.

Work the piece of knitting to the point where you change needle size. Then put aside the free needle and begin the next row with the new-size needle. At the end of that row, drop the free needle and work the following row with the second new needle.

ACKNOWLEDGMENTS

We would like to extend our gratitude and special thanks to the following designers who contributed projects to this book.

Charlotte Biro with Beverly
  Rivers—29
Charlotte Biro—53
Gary Boling—11,46–47,
  48–49, 52
Bucilla Yarn Company—12–13
Barbara Chamberlain with
  Glenda Dawson—4–5
Coats and Clark—26–27, 50
  (designed by Dixie Falls, adapt-
  ed for crochet by Coats and
  Clark)
Glenda Dawson with Barbara
  Chamberlain—4–5
Susan Douglas—30–31
Dixie Falls—54–55, 56
Suzette Fell—7
Kathy Ferneau—51
Juanita King for Knit Wits of
  Iowa—25
Gail Kinkead—57
Janet McCaffery—28
Beverly Rivers with Charlotte
  Biro—29
Clara Storm—10
Nancy Taylor—8–9
Erna Toomsen for Knit Wits of
  Iowa—58–59 (knitted fisher-
  man afghan)
Sara Jane Treinen—6, 20–21,
  22–23, 24, 58–59 (fisherman
  crochet afghan)

For their cooperation and courtesy, we extend a special thanks to the following sources for providing materials for projects.

Berger du Nord
  Brookman & Sons, Inc.
  4416 NE. 11th Ave.
  Ft. Lauderdale, FL 33334

Bernat Yarn & Craft Corp.
  Depot & Mendon Sts.
  Uxbridge, MA 05169

Brunswick Yarns
  Brunswick Ave.
  P.O. Box 548
  Moosup, CT 06354

Bucilla Co.
  150 Meadowlands Pkwy.
  P.O. Box 1534
  Secaucus, NY 07094

Coats & Clark, Inc.
  72 Cummings Rd.
  Stamford, CT 06904

Laines Anny Blatt
  24770 Crestview
  Farmington Hills, MI 48018

Pingouin Corp.
  P.O. Box 100
  Jamestown, SC 29453

C.M. Offray & Son, Inc.
  261 Madison Ave.
  New York, NY 10016

Ultex, Inc.
  21 Adley Rd.
  Cambridge, MA 02138

William Unger & Co., Inc.
  230 Millwood Rd.
  Chappaqua, NY 10514

We are also pleased to acknowledge the following photographers, whose talents and technical skills contributed much to this book.

Mike Dieter—24, 29, 30–31,
  46–47, 50, 53, 54 (detail), 57,
  72–79
Jim Hedrich—4–5
Thomas Hooper—12–13
Scott Little—7, 8 (detail), 10,
  21 (detail), 26–27
Sid Spelts—8–9, 20–21, 51, 52,
  54–55, 56
Jim Kascoutas—11, 22–23,
  25, 28